"Bash Dibra leads u

the human-canine r

work, but *how we can make it work.*"

—Roger Caras, President, ASPCA

"He doesn't train your dog; he trains you to train your dog by thinking like a dog."

—*In Style*

"Bash Dibra has such a cult following among Manhattan pet owners that he is known simply as Bash, like a rock star. . . . To clients like Alec Baldwin, he's 'top dog' among personal pet trainers."

—*The New York Times*

"High profile folks like Mariah Carey and Henry Kissinger rely on Bash, the trainer who can turn the most problematic pooch into a model canine."

—*W*

"Bash did a great job in training Sally, our Border Collie, and in return, she absolutely adores him. That, to me, seems like the best endorsement of his training philosophy."

—Matthew Broderick

"Anyone who can teach Spike *anything* should be sainted."

—Joan Rivers

"I think Bash Dibra was raised by wolves." —Nancy Friday

"Bash Dibra is recognized as an authority and deservedly so."

—William J. Kay, DVM, Animal Medical Center

"There's nobody quite like Bash when it comes to dogs! Within a few weeks my two Bichons were behaving perfectly and trotting happily on their leashes."

—Barbara Taylor Bradford

"Bash not only trains dogs, but truly loves them. And they love him too."

—Sarah Jessica Parker

"Bash is as much a dog psychiatrist as a trainer. His ongoing commitment to animals is truly inspiring."

—Victoria (Mrs. S. I.) Newhouse

Bash Dibra

with Mary Ann Crenshaw

Illustrations by José Dennis

Simon & Schuster

DogSpeak

How to Learn It, Speak It, and Use It to Have a Happy, Healthy, Well-Behaved Dog

SIMON & SCHUSTER
Rockefeller Center
1230 Avenue of the Americas
New York, NY 10020

Designed by DEIRDRE C. AMTHOR

Manufactured in the United States of America

10 9 8 7 6 5 4 3

Library of Congress Cataloging-in-Publication Data

Dibra, Bashkim.
Dogspeak : how to learn it, speak it, and use it to develop a happy, healthy, well-behaved dog / Bash Dibra ; with Mary Ann Crenshaw ; illustrations by José Dennis.
p. cm.
1. Dogs—Behavior. 2. Dogs—Training. 3. Human-animal communication. I. Crenshaw, Mary Ann. II. Title.
SF433.D53 1999
636.7'0887—dc21 99-30194
CIP

ISBN 0-684-82417-5

Acknowledgments

There is no way I can express my gratitude to those whose patience and understanding supported me throughout the writing of this book—my family, my friends, my clients. Special thanks go to my sister Meruet, who took over all business matters while I was "otherwise engaged," and to my sister Hope, who always is there for me. Thanks as well to my creative editor, Fred Hills, for keeping the book, and me, so clearly focused.

And to all the animals in my life—past, present, and future—I am deeply indebted, but most especially to Mariah the wolf, whose spirit remains a part of me and, I hope, with you, within the pages of this book.

Bash Dibra
New York, NY
February 1999

This book is dedicated to all dog owners
who understand and appreciate
the unconditional love and joy a dog brings to life.

Contents

Introduction: How It Began

My earliest childhood memories are of barbed wire, guards, crowded rooms, and fear. As a five-year-old, I had no comprehension of my circumstances . . . that my parents had made a courageous decision to flee the tyranny of Communism in our homeland, Albania . . . that their decision had led us to this place, a Yugoslavian internment camp where day-to-day life meant hardship and cold, hunger and fear, insecurity and despair. I do remember the weeping, the sadness, and my own confusion as my family huddled in a tiny jaillike room with no comforts and, apparently, no way out.

Outside, however, there was fresh air, sunlight, breezes, and the sounds of birds, free as all nature, singing happily. And there was something else that fascinated me: the four-legged creatures that patrolled the perimeter of the camp with the guards. These animals had a mysterious air about them, as if they knew something I needed to know. As if they had the secret to why, when, and where. I felt drawn to them, curious to know how it would feel to touch their thick fur, to look into their dark eyes. And I kept being drawn to that part of the camp where these creatures had their enclosure, where they slept and ate, free from the restraints of the guards. Typical of any five-year-old, I was curious, I was fearless, and I was innocent. No one had ever explained to me that these were ferocious guard dogs, trained to attack—to kill, if necessary—to keep those of us inside from getting out. And so, one day, I walked up to the fence of their enclosure and stuck my fist through the wire. As horrified guards watched from afar, one of the dogs approached. At that moment, I instinctively opened my fist and extended my hand. The big dog lowered his head, sniffed, and then gave my hand a lick. By the time the guards came running, I had made a friend.

The guards were stunned and quickly removed me from the area, taking me into their office, where they questioned me on why I was there, what I was doing. Didn't I know that the dogs could have killed me? They sent for my parents and interrogated them, warning that they must keep me away from these animals. And in case we didn't get their message, they put on their protective gear and gave a vivid and terrifying demonstration of how a guard dog attacks and what damage it can do. My parents were distraught, furious with me, terrified of what could have happened and terrified of what repercussions my behavior might elicit. There was a great deal of yelling, crying, and snarling, as I sat there, completely confused. I had angered both the people who loved me, my parents, and the people I feared, the guards. And yet, somehow, fear wasn't the message the dog had given me. Somehow I had the very deep feeling that dogs and I—no matter what my parents and the guards were saying—could be friends.

For days I was kept indoors, well away from the dogs' area. My parents and the camp guards were, for once, allies. But still I was drawn back to the animals' area, convinced that these big, beautiful animals were not as evil and vicious as everyone was telling me. And when no one was looking, once again I stuck my fist through the fence. The dogs began snarling, barking, showing very large teeth, but when I opened my hand, once again they approached, sniffed, and gave me a lick. I knew, once and for all, that these were my friends.

And so, finally, did the guards, who, somewhat mystified by the animals' response to me, decided it might be better, for camp control, simply to let me remain with them, in the guards' quarters. At least from there, they could supervise my behavior.

For the next three years, the guards, the dogs, and I established a ritual: I could visit the dogs, but I had to go through the guards' quarters so that the other internees couldn't see me. It would have been bad for morale for me to have more freedom than anyone else. But in fact, I did. The dogs had guaranteed my passport to freedom, to a new life outside the fence, to a new life with nature, a yearning that was being satisfied. A sense of hope. Meanwhile, with my newfound friends (including the guards, who now seemed less intimidating and much, much nicer), each day held new adventures, new and exciting experiences. And before I knew it, I was beginning to grow up.

When I was old enough to understand such things, a holy man in the camp told me a story. It's a story I've never forgotten and it reflects my own feelings about dogs.

"You are very lucky, Bash," he told me, "that you've had this amazing experience with animals. The relationship that we have with dogs—this bond we feel—is a gift from God. And it comes from a time in the far, far past, when man lived in the garden, and it was a very beautiful world. Man and nature were in unison in this very special place, where man and animals lived in harmony and could talk together, each in his own language. All understood one another perfectly and life was beautiful. It was nothing at all like this camp.

"But one day man broke God's rules, and God was very, very angry. He gathered all of the animals in the garden and told them that because man had broken the rules, he would have to leave the garden. However, being a merciful God, he asked that one animal remain by man's side. The world outside of the garden was a very frightening and lonely place; God wouldn't be there to protect man, who would need a friend. All the animals looked at one another and not one said a word. Finally a wolf stepped forward and stood next to the man. And when the man and the wolf stepped through the gate of the garden into the wide world outside, the wolf was transformed into a dog. Man and dog have been best friends ever since."

It wasn't until I was much older—grown, in fact—that I recognized one irrefutable fact, a fact which would revolutionize my training methods and change my life forever. It was this: The dog has evolved from the wolf, and the relationship that was formed there in the garden exists between man and dog to this day. After all, "dog" spelled backwards is "God."

In my life, dogs have been the greatest gift I ever could have received. I hope that this book will allow you to experience the great joy of knowing and communicating with a dog. I promise that doing so will create a bond so strong, even death cannot break it.

DogSpeak

Chapter 1

Discovering DogSpeak

Do you know, because he's told you, when your dog has to go out . . . *now?* Do you understand, because he's shown you, when he isn't feeling up to a run today? And do you guess, without his telling you, that when he sees you leave each morning, he's afraid you'll never come home again—and can you reassure him that this isn't true? If the answer is "yes," then you're already ahead of the game. You already understand dog language. If not, then welcome to the wonderful world of DogSpeak and the most rewarding relationship you'll ever experience in life.

When you think about it, dogs are incredible creatures. In a short time, they can learn an amazing amount of our human language. (Standard poodles are said to have a vocabulary of some 300 words!) They have the capacity to intuit our moods, read our facial expressions, and even find meaning in our body language. So imagine how they feel when we don't do the same for them. If you've ever tried to make yourself understood in a foreign country where no one spoke your language and you couldn't understand theirs, you know the frustration. I wonder whether dogs sometimes view us humans as a bit backward, or whether they are just more eager to please.

One thing I learned about dogs early in life: They are pure and honest creatures—honest about themselves, pure in their affections, open about their likes and dislikes. If you treat them with kindness and *respect,* they are your friends for life, offering you the unconditional love that most humans can't even comprehend. Unfortunately, too many of us can't take advantage of the extraordinary gift our dogs offer us, because *we don't understand their language* (and probably have no idea how to learn it). Yet it's a language as old as time, dating back to that prehistoric era when humans and wolves first became partners, moving from competition to the mutual benefits of cooperation. Man quickly learned that the wolf could be an effective "watchdog" against other predators; wolves, once they'd been on the receiving end of man's prehistoric table scraps, soon learned that this was easier than hunting. This new relationship spawned its own unspoken language, clear, simple, and direct, and the bond created has survived to this day, evolving into the extraordinary and quite unique friendship that exists between man and the wolf's direct descendants, dogs. It's one of the strongest bonds in human history.

But where our ancestors had a vested interest in speaking wolf language—their own survival!—we modern-day humans, for the most part, have lost their ability to communicate with dogs in their own language, a language I call DogSpeak. As a result, we miss out on experiencing the wonderful synergy that occurs when dog and master think alike, act in unison, and live in complete harmony with one another. If you've ever witnessed an experienced shepherd work his sheep dogs, you'll understand what I mean. And yet DogSpeak isn't a difficult, prehistoric language; it's vitally alive, crystal clear, remarkably expressive, and, for those who choose to learn it, incredibly easy. All that's required is patience, a little effort, and the willingness to listen to your dog.

When I became a trainer, I already knew I had a unique and instinctive bond with dogs. That had been demonstrated by my childhood experiences with guard dogs. Perhaps, coming as it did in my early, formative years, that experience tapped into the innate, intuitive abilities that exist deep within us all but are lost to most of us through centuries of neglect. (Fortunately, working with animals is the quickest way to regain this "sixth sense.") Somehow, as a child, I automatically sensed how to work with and manage "unmanageable" dogs. Nonetheless, once I'd grown up and decided to make a career of working with animals, I studied with the best trainers in Europe to learn those scientifically proven techniques that are the cornerstone of any trainer's basic education, ultimately developing a career that has been both successful and fulfilling. But it wasn't until I met Mariah, a timber wolf pup, that I learned there was much more to the canine/human relationship than simple obedience. There was communication on a level I'd never even dreamed existed.

When I was given the assignment of training a wolf for a film role, I knew that I wanted to understand more about wolves and how they communicate. Of course I'd studied their behavior as part of my education and even had worked with adult wolves during my apprenticeship. This was different. This time it was entirely up to me and I needed to know everything I could about these magnificent creatures, including the dynamics of pack behavior, that genetically coded and highly complicated social structure that governs every aspect of the wolf's interactions. For that reason, I thought it would be best to begin with a pup. I could imprint myself on it from infancy, become its pack leader and be that far ahead in the training game. And since wolves are the ancestors of dogs, if I really understood wolf behavior—which part of it was genetically coded, which the result of environment—I would gain tremendous insight into the thought processes of dogs, an invaluable aid in my work as a trainer.

But I knew I'd need to choose my wolf pup carefully. I also knew I wanted a female. Males of most species generally are more aggressive. Knowing the ongoing battle for dominance among members of the wolf pack (a behavior that also exists with dogs) and also knowing that if this were to be a successful relationship, my maintaining the upper hand was key—I needed to establish my authority early on. A female probably would accept more readily my position as Alpha leader of our pack of two.

At a wolf sanctuary in Maine, I found my wolf, choosing her exactly the way I would choose any pup: by observing the interactions of the pups within the litter, watching for signs of aggression, fearfulness, oversubmissiveness, or any other qualities that might be undesirable. I held each pup on its back. If it responded aggressively by growling or snapping, I knew it wasn't the pup for me. I needed one that would accept me as the dominant Alpha figure in its life. A pup that would relax in my arms would indicate just the right amount of submissiveness to an Alpha. I finally chose one, Mariah. She would be my pup, I would be her Alpha. What was important now was to begin the imprinting process, assuring her acceptance of this human creature on whom, now, her very life depended.

While Mariah was being weaned, I visited the sanctuary daily and fed her from a bottle, accustoming her to my presence and my scent. Soon she would leave her wolf family—a traumatizing experience for any animal, but especially so for extremely pack-responsive wolves—and travel to New York, where she would learn a new way of life, far from the wild but to her twice as fearsome.

At six weeks, Mariah was ready to make the transition from wolf pup to house pup. I loaded her into a traveling crate, packed her into my station wagon, and off we went to begin our adventurous new life together. It was quite a transition for us both. Like any pup newly removed from the comforting presence of her mother, Mariah was frightened.

She didn't understand this strange new world, where every sound was different, every smell foreign and possibly dangerous, and all of it fearsome. Once we'd arrived at my house and I'd removed Mariah from her traveling crate and placed her on the floor, she was terrified. In order to reassure her, I had prepared a crate (a cage) in my bedroom that would serve as her "den." I knew the importance of this safe haven, a place where she could feel secure. But once inside the crate, Mariah refused to come out, despite my coaxing. I tempted her by placing a bowl of food just inside her crate, then slowly withdrawing it. Finally, both hungry and thirsty, Mariah tentatively emerged from her "den," gobbled down the food ("wolfed down" took on new meaning for me!), and lapped a bit of water. I remained quiet, observing as she began, cautiously and nervously, to explore this new environment, all of it so strange to her. I remained as still as possible while she adjusted to this odd new place. After about forty-five minutes, I slipped on a collar and light leash. At the first touch of it, Mariah froze, still as a statue, the traditional response of a frightened wolf. (The theory seems to be "If I'm still, perhaps they won't know I'm here.") I let her remain in that position for as long as she needed, then finally picked her up, stroked her, and walked her on-leash outdoors. It was the first important step in the most important training lesson of my life, the beginning of my understanding those wolf behaviors that led to DogSpeak.

Once outside, Mariah reverted to her frozen stance, a natural thing for wild animals and a defense mechanism against fear, but after a bit of encouragement on my part she began to walk around and explore the yard, sniffing the grass, the trees, the strange odors. Within minutes, she urinated (by now she'd been holding it a very long time for a pup), marking her new environment. This was an important step for us both, since on each subsequent trip outdoors, she would catch her own scent and immediately feel secure. Wolves use urine to establish the boundaries of their turf and their uncanny ability to read scents makes these urine-markings a primary form of communication. It's an ability passed down genetically to your dog, which is why urine-marking is a common form of DogSpeak communication.

Back inside the house, I continued to stroke her, holding her and speaking to her soothingly until she reverted to her freezing stance, telling me she'd had enough. Then I returned her to her crate/den, this time closing and locking the door, for her security and safety as well as a beginning to the housebreaking process. Soon Mariah would learn that the only acceptable place to relieve herself was outdoors, in the yard that she now had marked as her own.

Can you imagine housebreaking a wolf? Fortunately, I understood the concept of den behavior. Wolves, like most animals, like to keep their dens clean. It's the last place they want to use for a bathroom. I already had created a "den" with the crate; now we had a bathroom schedule we both could depend on. It was vital to our future relationship, and her training process, that Mariah know she could count on me to take her out of her crate to eat, play, exercise, *and* go to the bathroom—the role her mother would have played in the wild. But while Mariah was dependent on me, and her total dependency was essential, I was *responsible* for her and I took my responsibilities seriously, as any animal owner must do. It was this relationship of dependency and responsibility that would create a singular bond between us, making us a pack of two, with me as the leader of that small pack. This was a relationship Mariah's

DNA had programmed her to expect. And it's also the relationship that will, in turn, create an unbreakable bond between you and your dog.

Mariah's housebreaking schedule consisted of walks outside every four hours. It didn't make for many restful nights, but I diligently kept up the schedule for the next three weeks, finally extending the time to six hours between walks. Mariah never had an "accident," never messed her den. Now she felt more secure outdoors, where, with each visit, her scent grew stronger. Mariah the wolf was housebroken!

About five days after Mariah had arrived, I introduced her to my other dogs. She already had caught their scent, knew they were there, and was becoming increasingly curious. They, on the other hand, were equally sure that there was some strange kind of creature in the house, something with a decidedly different odor. It was time for the dogs to meet their new wolf sister, and Mariah her new "littermates," in the appropriate manner. I presented each dog to Mariah individually, placing them in the Down/Stay position while Mariah approached and sniffed. Occasionally I asked the dog to lie on its side, a submissive posture that in both wolf language and DogSpeak indicates acceptance. Soon the dogs and the wolf were accepting of each other though, invariably, when my dogs would begin to lick her (the standard greeting between both wolves and dogs), Mariah would roll onto her back in submission, clearly saying to them, "Don't hurt me, I'm just a little girl." Apparently her DogSpeak was impeccable and my dogs got her message. Mariah, in turn, was reassured by the presence of these furry creatures, with whom she was far more comfortable than those still-strange humans.

As Mariah grew, each day bigger, stronger, and more beautiful, I studied and learned to read the many facial expressions and body gestures that she, and all wolves, exhibit, comparing them to the amazingly similar gestures and expressions of my dogs. It was clear that the ancestral lines of communication had remained open and that the wolf had passed its heritage down to its descendants, domestic dogs. The more I observed those similarities, the more I realized that the driving force that governs all wolf behavior, the Code of the Pack, had found its way down the genetic line to encode the behavior of all dogs as well. Don't get me wrong: I am not one of those who believes that dogs can't think. I've seen too much in my career that tells me they not only think, but *feel,* on a very deep level. But I also began to realize that no amount of socialization, of human companionship, can completely override the dog's genetic makeup, that complex and highly organized behavior that is its heritage. And I began to see that to work successfully in training Mariah, I'd need to train *within* this deeply imprinted code, to combine the behavior the wolf was born to exhibit with behavior that was socially acceptable in the civilized world.

I studied pack behavior more carefully, and watched Mariah even more closely for its manifestations—signs of instincts so deeply imbedded they'd be difficult to erase. Even though she'd been removed from her pack at an early age, certain wolflike behaviors—territoriality, food guarding, flight response—already were impacting the training process. Soon I had isolated certain factors of pack behavior that affected every aspect of our relationship and which were amazingly similar to certain behaviors of my own dogs. Clearly these factors were basic to both species, and if I understood and worked *with* them, rather than against them, I could not only understand the complex behavior of the wolf but of all its dog descendants. Little did I realize that I was on my way to developing a revolutionary theory of dog training, based on these Eight Central Factors of Pack Behavior.

The Eight Central Factors of Pack Behavior

1. The Dominance Hierarchy. The success of a wolf pack—how it lives, hunts, breeds, and socializes as a family unit—depends on one thing: a strong Alpha leader. He (or she) is the wolf who calls the shots, determines the social hierarchy within the pack, decides who goes where, who eats and when, and even who can remain a member of the pack. Every other wolf within the pack must remain submissive to this autocratic leader. Yet since his position is challenged on a daily basis by would-be Alphas, the Alpha must keep his pack under tight control and doesn't hesitate to use force to protect his dominant position. While this arrangement may sound unpleasant to us humans, it offers wolves a social structure that assures safety, security, and continuity for the entire pack.

Typically a pack is led by an Alpha male, which dominates all other males, and an Alpha female, which dominates females (as a rule, this Alpha couple is the pack's breeding pair). The rest of the pack is arranged in a descending hierarchy, all of it rigidly controlled. (Though packs normally are led by a male Alpha, Alpha females also may become pack leaders and *always* decide where the pack dens, and therefore where it hunts.) In other words, a wolf pack is a highly functional family. That's the relationship you want with your dog—you as Alpha, your dog as obedient Beta. But like the Alpha wolf, you, the Alpha leader, may be challenged every day by your rebellious pet, especially if he has strong Alpha aspirations (you'll soon learn how to spot those through DogSpeak). It's simply dog nature, and it's remarkably similar to the behavior of toddlers. Stand firm and remember that if you're not the Alpha calling the shots, nobody will feel secure—including you.

2. Aggression. Aggression is necessary for a wolf's survival. It helps pack members establish their territory, maintain their rank in the pack hierarchy, protect their food supply, and drive away would-be predators. It's a deeply ingrained instinct. But in our socialized world, aggression is unacceptable behavior and there's absolutely no place for it in the life of a domestic dog. At the first sign of real aggression, you, the Alpha/owner, *must* step in and stop the problem before there are serious consequences. Don't worry. When you've learned DogSpeak, you'll know immediately how to spot the warning signals and stop aggression before it begins.

3. Territorial Behavior. Territorial behavior is used by wolves to mark their "turf," giving clear warning to other packs that "this is home—you stay out!" Territorial behavior is displayed by urinating to mark the pack's boundaries, barking to alert to intruders, and using aggression to keep intruders at bay. Sound familiar? Your own dog exhibits this behavior each time it barks when a stranger approaches your property, urinates to mark its neighborhood, or growls if another dog approaches its master or the boundaries of its home territory. He's protecting you in DogSpeak, and that's good within limits. But if territorial behavior turns into aggression towards strangers or other dogs, or urinating in the house to mark its territory, it's no, no, *no!*

4. Food Guarding. If a wolf doesn't protect its food, it goes without. Easy to understand, then, why food guarding is such a deeply ingrained instinct, one your dog has imprinted deep within its genetic makeup. It's natural behavior, and when there are several canine family members, it's perfectly acceptable for a dog to be protective of his food. But exhibiting aggressive food guarding toward you or any family member is completely unacceptable and *must be stopped immediately.* I'll teach you how to do that with DogSpeak.

5. Flight Behavior. Wolves have extraordinarily keen eyesight, with highly developed peripheral vision, which makes them quick to perceive even the slightest movement around them. Thus, at the first sign of danger, or when something unknown rushes towards them, they instinctively flee. It's a case of flight or fight, with flight seeming the more sensible choice. (As a rule, wolves are pacifists.) But the same behavior that serves to protect wolves can have just the opposite result for dogs and if your dog takes off like a shot at a loud noise or a newspaper blown by the wind, he may be headed for real danger—into the path of an onrushing car, for instance. That's why you, the strong Alpha/owner, must keep your dog *always on leash* and entirely under control. It's the only sure way to keep you both safe and confident. Trust me: Your dog needs to know that you, his Alpha, are in charge and that he can relax!

6. Chase Behavior. With their keen vision, wolves automatically pursue anything that runs away from them, giving no quarter in the hunt. To chase and hunt down prey is a genetically imprinted instinct that means survival for those animals who must hunt to eat. Even though they may have their food served up in a china bowl, dogs still have that deeply ingrained instinct to chase down anything that runs. It's why they love to chase sticks, retrieve balls, and play hide-and-seek. However, if your dog decides to pursue joggers, bicycles, skaters, or even a running child, there could be serious consequences. This is one instinct you must keep under strict control, particularly if your dog is large and powerful.

7. Socialization. Wolves have an extraordinary sense of fun, and play is an integral part of their social structure. They are astonishing in their friendliness towards other members of the pack, greeting each other effusively with licks, usually around the face and muzzle, each time they meet. It's the lupine version of a social kiss! Wolves always take time for play (something we humans would do well to emulate), making it an essential part of pack life. Dogs, just like wolves, not only love to play but *need* to, and any dog who is kept isolated from canine or human companionship, who never enjoys a game of toss-the-ball or tug-the-bone or experiences the joy of a playful relationship with its owner, will be an unhappy dog indeed. With unhappiness come problems such as destructiveness, excessive barking, even aggression, all signs of boredom and discontent. So each time your dog greets you with licks and wags and brings you his ball to toss, please acknowledge it appropriately. He's telling you clearly, in DogSpeak, that dogs just want to have fun!

8. Vocalization. In their social world, wolves love to chat. They whine, yip, bark, and howl to communicate with one another in language that is perfectly understood by all wolves and conveys happiness, loneliness, concern, fear, and warnings. Often it's a bark that says "Hi, I'm here," or a lone wolf's howl that means "I'm lonely, come find me," or even a warning growl that says "Don't come any closer!" Every pitch, every sound carries a crystal-clear meaning to other wolves, who respond appropriately. Even that eerie chorus of howls that has chilled the hearts of man for centuries usually is nothing more than a joyous wolf "sing." Your dog loves to vocalize as well, and by the time you're fluent in DogSpeak, you'll be able to distinguish every nuance of his speech. Vocalization is natural and fine, within limits. But nobody loves a constantly barking or unnecessarily whiny dog. Teaching your dog acceptable limits is up to you, the Alpha/owner, and enforcing them will guarantee a much more peaceful lifestyle for you, your neighbors, and your pet.

• • •

Once I understood the Eight Central Factors of Pack Behavior that wolves and dogs have in common, I looked at my own dogs in a somewhat different light. It was easy to see the "why" for their sometimes peculiar habits, easy to be more tolerant of behaviors that they really were born to exhibit. They honestly couldn't help it. And yet, I'd trained them to behave as responsible social creatures, accepted in all the best places for their impeccable behavior. I was going to have to work the same miracle on Mariah, except now I'd view it all from an entirely different perspective, that of the wolf. I had no desire to take the wolf out of Mariah, but if she were to become a movie star, I couldn't permit her to indulge in any antisocial behaviors. Food guarding, howling, and aggression might not be considered antisocial in the wild—in fact, they all would be quite necessary to survival—but in Hollywood? Probably not!

As the months went by (and they flew!), Mariah and I became a team, one that could communicate within our own closed society and in the world outside our home. In other words, I learned to speak wolf language. And the longer I lived with Mariah, the more struck I was by the similarities between her behavior and that of my dogs. It was as if she were dog in microcosm, the quintessential canine. To understand Mariah was to understand canine behavior, and to communicate with her, in her language, was the greatest gift I have ever received. It taught me to love, honor, and respect this magnificent species and, in return, gave me something beyond value: the ability to speak dog language. I intend to pass that ability along to you in *DogSpeak*.

Chapter 2

DogSpeak for Beginners

Dogs always keep things simple. Their communication with each other is clear, direct, and easily understood, with *no* mixed messages. It's the genetic heritage of their wolf ancestors, who depended for survival on a close-knit familial society in which every pack member communicated easily and immediately with every other member. The hierarchy was understood, as was the language that accompanied it, and when the Alpha gave a command, it was obeyed. So it is with dogs. Dogs never misinterpret another's signals; humans often do, creating the problems that result in the dog's being abandoned or banished to a shelter and the euthanasia that often follows. And that's truly tragic, since dog language is precise in its meaning, clear in its message, and easy to speak, once you've learned its vocabulary. I am here to help you do that, to guide you into the mind of a dog and help you explore its unique abilities, its subtle signals, the remarkable ways in which a dog uses its entire range of senses and virtually every part of its body to express its thoughts, moods, needs, and emotions.

Seeing Your Dog for the First Time

First, please set aside all preconceived notions about dogs and how they communicate and examine their signals in a new and different light, seeing them as your dog does. You should be as alert, intense, and aware as your dog, and the best way to achieve that is by observing him. What's he saying to you right now? Are his ears pricked up, curious to know why you're watching him? Or are they lowered and slightly slanted as he looks up from his bed to see what you have in mind? Can you read his eyes? Are they bright with anticipation, sparkling with delight, or perhaps half-closed, indicating he's a bit unsure about this sudden interest in him? Does his mouth seem to smile, or does it have a sad expression? Is his tail wagging wildly, lowered and relaxed, or tucked between his legs apprehensively? With every one of these signals, your dog is telling you something. I know that many people scoff at the very idea that a dog exhibits many of the same emotions as people. I might too, if I hadn't spent my entire life around dogs whose vast range of expressions taught me that what I see is what they feel.

Dogs speak to us humans plainly and clearly in their language. It's up to us to hear them. When you've learned DogSpeak, you'll know exactly, by his gestures, his sounds, and his facial expressions, what your dog is saying. You'll know whether he's happy or depressed, energetic or under-the-weather, lonely, frightened or on top of the canine world. By observing closely the body language, facial expressions, and gestures that are DogSpeak, you will be able to communicate with your dog on a new and higher level. Then you're free to listen in on your dog's canine conversations, look over his shoulder as he sniffs out messages on the doggie Internet, understand which dogs are his friends and which he perceives as his enemies (useful knowledge for heading off potential problems), and assume your rightful role as the Alpha of your family pack. And once you're fluent in DogSpeak, you and your dog will develop the unique, unbreakable, and enviable bond that makes the dog/owner relationship the strongest, most enduring relationship on earth.

Where DogSpeak Began

Before there was DogSpeak, there was the eloquent language of wolves, who depended on all of their highly developed senses for survival. Their senses of smell and hearing alerted them to prey as well as to danger. Vocalization was used as an alert call, a plea for help, a warning, a lonely wail, a statement of status, or a highly social group chorus. A clear and readily understood body language established and maintained the pack hierarchy. All of these same hyperacute senses, passed down from wolves to your dog, make up the vocabulary and grammar of DogSpeak. In order for you to understand what your dog is saying, you first must understand the sensory components that make his language possible, some of them so evolved as to be nearly incomprehensible to us mere humans.

Just like wolves, dogs communicate in a language that every other dog understands perfectly. They use their keen sight, their extraordinary sense of smell, their hypersensitive ears, their eloquent voices, their responsive muscles, their skin, and even their hormones and glands to convey the most subtle nuances of meaning. Dogs also have an exquisitely tuned sixth sense that lets them intuit, long before the actual signal is sent, what's coming. Have you ever studied your dog as he was sleeping? Did you find it remarkable that he usually awakened and looked at you as if to say, "Yes? What's up?" If you haven't, try it sometime and witness a perfect example of how dogs pick up on signals we haven't really delivered, the result of intuition developed by their wolf ancestors eons ago as a protective device. (It helps to know when a predator is in the vicinity!) This uncanny sixth sense is at work when your dog seems to know the exact time you're due to arrive from the office, or senses your approach while you're still blocks away. There are countless documented cases of dogs who could time, to the minute, when their masters or mistresses would walk in the front door. I have a client who tells me her dog knows when I am entering her building, even though she lives on the thirty-first floor. We humans could profit considerably by this intuition and, I'm happy to say, we can develop it to a large degree by tuning in to, and communicating with, our dogs. First, we must begin with the canine equivalent of the alphabet, with me and your dog as interpreters. I'll show you the meaningful gestures, expressions, sounds, and postures that make up the language called DogSpeak. After that, we'll explore the fascinating dialects that make one breed's "accent" slightly different from another's, as well as the subtle differences that occur from dog to dog. But first things first. Let's begin by learning a new alphabet—the one that will make you the Alpha. The best way to do that is to begin where DogSpeak began: with the language of wolves.

Primal DogSpeak, the Language of Wolves

The language of wolves is many-faceted, yet crystal clear to any other wolf *or* to any one of its canine descendants. To understand this complex language, one first must understand just how wolves use not only every one of their senses but their skin, their glands, their muscles, and virtually all of their bodies to convey amazingly precise meanings. When you understand the acuity of a wolf's (and a dog's) sensory system, you'll undoubtedly develop new respect for them and the language they speak.

The Sense of Smell

The olfactory center is the most developed part of a wolf's brain, as it is of your dog's, and it's where DogSpeak begins. A wolf's acute sense of smell lets it identify airborne scents from a distance of several miles and alerts to the presence of prey (the next meal) as well as to their only dangerous enemy, man. The sensitive nose of the wolf can track its prey through the animal's scent on freshly crushed vegetation or can locate an injured animal through the scent of just one drop of its blood. Wolves even can pursue prey *through water,* using as little as a single drop of urine or blood within 10,000 gallons of water to stay on track. This keen nose, by the way, has been bred selectively into today's scent hounds.

Wolves use their highly developed sense of smell in social ways as well. Within their pack setting, wolves can recognize, by their unmistakable scents, each and every member of their pack, distinguishing them from intruding members of other packs. It's a faculty which helps maintain established boundaries, allowing no interlopers. Their keen noses tell them when females are in season or when a fellow pack member is ill and wants to be left alone. And when the Alpha female produces a litter, each pack member sniffs every pup, imprinting permanently on their consciousness the scent that says "I'm one of you." This remarkable olfactory sense is genetically hard-wired into your own dog, making up the most developed center of the brain and controlling, to a great degree, your dog's behavior.

The olfactory center of a dog's brain is fourteen times larger than man's, making its nose a hundred times more sensitive. Wolves can recognize scents at a mile and a half downwind! Dogs, like wolves, can detect substances in concentrations up to *100 million times lower* than what humans can detect. Understanding the mind of your dog means acknowledging a sense of smell so highly developed and formidable that it is almost incomprehensible to us humans. But for dogs, it's just the *A* in the DogSpeak alphabet.

The Sense of Hearing

Some scientists believe that wolves track large prey more by sound than by smell. The wolf's range of hearing, coupled with its keen powers of auditory discrimination, make hearing its most powerful sense. Research has shown that wolves can hear sounds up to a high frequency of twenty-six kilohertz, well beyond human hearing and close to the range of bats. Their ability to detect these high-pitched sounds lets wolves locate small prey such as rodents, even under snow packs, by sounding out their high-pitched squeals. Wolves can hear and identify a fellow wolf's howls from a distance of more than four miles. The wolf's highly sensitive hearing, with its equally developed sense of smell, make up the two most important tools to the survival of the wolf species. It's this same finely tuned auditory sense that lets your dog hear thunder from miles away (ever see him hide under a bed long before a storm struck?), bark protectively at an outdoor sound you can't hear at all, or pick up another dog's low growl that is undetectable to you. It's also this keen sense of hearing that makes your dog a valuable protector of your home.

The Sense of Sight

A wolf's vision was designed for efficiency. With fewer and less concentrated color cones (those sensory organs of the retina that govern both color and close vision) than the human eye, a wolf's eye perceives color less vividly than humans and doesn't see detail in close-up objects. Instead, the wolf's eye was designed for extraordinary clarity and definition both in low light and at great distances, allowing it to move easily by night and track its prey by the slightest motion—the twitch of a rabbit's tail, the tremble of a leaf that betrays the squirrel.

Since visual cues are an essential element of body language, the wolf's keen sense of sight allows it to read accurately the pack status, moods, or intentions of other wolves. This acute visual sense, coupled with the wolf's speed, was passed down to domestic dogs and used by breeders to develop what we know today as "sight hounds"—hounds that spot and bring down prey primarily through their extraordinary sense of sight and their enormous speed. It is through your dog's visual senses that the two of you can communicate most effectively in DogSpeak. The visual cues that your dog gives you are the key to what he is seeing, recognizing, focusing on, and responding to. Just as with humans, his eyes are the windows to his interior universe, and by looking into them and understanding what he's seeing and saying, you'll have your first and most important conversation in DogSpeak.

Vocalization

With wolves, vocalization serves a variety of needs: howls often represent a gala social pack "sing"; whines may indicate concern or discomfort or serve as a call for help; yips, growls, and barks alert to intruders, establish status according to pack hierarchy, let pack members stay in touch with each other even from a distance, and help lone wolves develop new packs with other loners. With their sharp sense of hearing and their ability to discern nuances in other wolves' sounds beyond human comprehension, wolves have developed a very vocal language that is understood clearly by all other wolves. In dogs, vocalization has evolved to another level. Certain breeds, such as hounds, have transformed the wolf's howl into a "bay," used to spur other hounds, as well as the hunter, into the chase. This same vocal message is given to you by your dog when he barks to get your attention, to say "Follow me!" For us, vocalization is the most obvious form of DogSpeak. To a dog, it's just one more grammatical tool.

Body Language

Long before dogs evolved, wolves had perfected a clear and easily understood body language. Using every highly developed sense at its disposal, the wolf used every part of its body, from muscular system to glandular system, to convey precisely to any other wolf its rank, territory, relationships, physical state, needs, and emotions. The wolf's eyes telegraphed dominance or submission, friendliness or aggression, suspicion, playfulness, pain, or just plain exhaustion. Ears stated clearly "Stranger approaching!," "Glad to see you!," or "We've found our prey!" The mouth, just like that of humans, parted lips in a "smile" or bared teeth in a universally recognized snarl. Meanwhile, the wolf used its stance to reinforce facial expressions ("I'm Alpha here, and don't you forget it!"), intimidate would-be interlopers, indicate a desire to play, or show romantic interest. The glandular system plays a part in territory marking. It's a language that is and remains, to this day, perfectly understood by your dog, the primal essence of DogSpeak. It's also the best possible place for you to begin learning to speak your dog's language! But first, let's get you the dog you *really* want.

Chapter 3

Getting the Dog You *Really* Want

Choosing a dog is a bit like choosing a marriage partner: You hope to find someone you can spend the rest of your life loving; someone compatible, whose lifestyle meshes with yours, whose habits and quirks, in your adoring eyes, seem delightful. In successful marriages, it's usually love first, then a period of adjustment, followed by a life together devoted to keeping the relationship happy and healthy. With a dog, it's much the same except that with a dog you have a monumental advantage: *You can know in advance what life with your canine partner will be* by selecting a breed whose DNA is programmed to mesh with your lifestyle. You can order up a big, powerful watch dog, a fun-loving athletic retriever, or a tiny, cuddlesome lap dog, knowing right up front what you'll get in the way of temperament, physical attributes, personality, even projected life span. (Too bad marrying isn't that easy!) Granted, dogs are as individual as people, which is why I find life with them so endlessly fascinating, but with the careful breeding that is done today, it's rare to find a dog that veers too far from its breed's standards. Since you're about to commit to a lifetime relationship just as serious as marriage, you owe it to yourself *and* your prospective four-footed mate to research all the possibilities available in the big, beautiful world of dogs, then make a considered, intelligent choice. It's essential to do your homework. Read, research, and learn everything there is to know about the breed you *think* you want. But before you do that, there's other research to do, this time about yourself. What I'd like to know is, are you really ready to own a dog?

Too many people buy a dog for all the wrong reasons—it's the "in" thing to do, they just couldn't resist that adorable little puppy in the pet shop, the children have been begging for a puppy or, worse yet, someone has given them a puppy as a gift (always a very bad idea). All too often such people have absolutely no idea what dog ownership entails and how it will impact their lives. When they find out, many simply dump the dogs as "a problem," adding yet another number to the staggering 15 million dogs abandoned or given up for adoption each and every year. Since becoming a dog owner is as serious a commitment as marriage or adopting a child (actually, it's a bit of both), it's not a relationship to be entered into lightly. Many of my clients say that if they had known what was involved in owning a dog, they'd never have gotten one. But then they always add, "I wouldn't change it for the world!" and go on to tell me about how their dog has transformed their lives. I believe *everyone* who likes dogs should own one—no other relationship offers so much unconditional love, no other relationship can improve life so dramatically. Yet if this is to be a long and happy relationship (the only kind we want), then it's important to understand, well in advance of the "marriage" contract, what's involved. We want this to be a happy partnership for both you *and* your four-footed mate. No divorces allowed!

Know Thyself

First, ask yourself some questions: Do you have room in your life for a dog? Not only space, but enough room in your *life* to give this relationship the attention and time it deserves. Can you make the necessary financial commitment? It's important to do research on the costs of veterinary care, boarding, and grooming. (One of my clients swears her poodle's beauty salon bills are higher than her own!) Can your work schedule accommodate the regular walks and exercise that every dog needs, or will the dog be left alone all day? If so, will you commit to a dog walker?

Are you only getting a dog to pacify the kids? Are they old enough to care for it? If not, how will you feel when the job of caring for it falls to you? Is there a new baby on the way? Any idea what it will mean to take care of *two* new babies at the same time?

What kind of a lifestyle do you lead? Are you a mover and doer who loves nothing more than a two-mile jog followed by an hour of Rollerblading, or are you a confirmed couch potato who thinks that a perfect evening is a good fire, a good book, and an early bedtime? Are you a big, strong man, a small-boned woman, or a retired person without all the energy you once had?

And what about your home: Do you live in a large house surrounded by an even larger yard or in a tiny studio apartment with no access to outdoor space? Is your home dogproof? Do you mind that your dog sheds or that your puppy tracks in mud? Is there room for that indispensable piece of equipment, a crate? Each of these factors will play a role in deciding which kind of dog is right for you.

Finally—and this is the most important question of all—are

you ready for a lifetime commitment? If not, perhaps you should wait until you are. A dog isn't a stuffed toy to be tossed away when it's no longer "fun." A dog is a living, breathing, *loving* creature that will devote its whole life to pleasing you. It deserves your commitment in return.

Research, Research, Research

Now's the time to begin your homework (you can't say the dog ate it . . . yet!) by making some up-front decisions about the kind of dog you want. If you've honestly considered your lifestyle, your space, your likes and dislikes, and your own physical condition, then you should have a pretty good idea by now of the type of dog you want (or should have), whether it's a rough-and-ready retriever or a pocket-size poodle. Now it's time to get more specific. If you long for a retriever to be your walking companion, then what sort of retriever? If you think a small dog would work best for you, then should you go for a Chihuahua or a Shih Tzu, or something in between? The range of choice is enormous, and the only way to make an intelligent decision is research, research, research. That involves reading everything you can find about the kind of dog you believe you want.

Seven Groups, Multiple Choices

Fortunately, the American Kennel Club (AKC) has made your work easier by dividing all purebred breeds into seven separate groups: Sporting Group, Herding Group, Working Group, Terrier Group, Hound Group, Toy Group, and Non-Sporting Group. Six of these groups consist of dogs bred for a specific purpose; one is made up of dogs whose purpose is no longer valid; each group has its own quite distinctive characteristics. Understanding more about those characteristics will help you make an intelligent decision about your dog-to-be. However, within each group are dozens of different breeds, each with its own set of personality traits and characteristics. Before you can make a final choice, you'll have more homework to do in order to select the most appropriate breed. When that's done, we can move to a lesson on how to select the best of your chosen breed. For now, let's take a look at some of your choices. Remember: You aren't the only one who needs a compatible mate—so does your dog. I believe that proper training can transform every dog into a well-mannered, socially acceptable pet, but if you want your dog to be *happy,* then go with genetics and opt for a dog bred to lead the kind of life you do. Asking a Maltese to act as a cattle dog is a stretch!

The Sporting Group

The Sporting Group is made up of breeds used by hunters in the field. This group includes pointers and setters, which point game for the hunter; retrievers, which do just that—retrieve the game and bring it to the hunter; and spaniels, which both flush and retrieve. Right away you know that a dog from the Sporting Group, whether it's the cuddlesome Cocker Spaniel or the laid-back Labrador, will be a dog that loves the outdoors, relishes a run, delights in chasing game, and loves to retrieve and return that game to its master. For a sporting dog, this isn't work, it's play, which is why a dog from the Sporting Group is a great choice for an active person who loves nature and the outdoors and likes to share that with a pet. If you're a person who loathes exercise and hates the outdoors, this definitely is the wrong dog for you. Sporting dogs like nothing better than a romp through the fields (don't be surprised to find a rabbit laid at your feet!) and they're usually up early and ready to go, go, go, expecting you to follow the same schedule. Late sleepers, be warned.

The Herding Group

It is in Herding Group dogs that one sees most clearly the dog's heritage from the wolf. Watch a sheep dog control a herd, crouching, watching, and moving it, and you'll see exactly how a wolf stalks and controls its prey. This herding instinct has been selectively bred for centuries to create dogs that are invaluable aides to farmers and ranchers. Since the interaction between the handler and dog is vitally important, herding dogs are bred to be alert and responsive to commands. To see them work is to see intelligence and beauty in action. Included in the Herding Group are English Sheep Dogs, Australian Cattle Dogs, Collies, Shetland Sheep Dogs, German Shepherd Dogs, Briards, Bouviers des Flandres, and Corgis. All are intelligent, agile, and athletic, supremely responsive and able to work on command or alone. If you're a person who likes action *and* interaction, and loves close communication with your dog, then these are a great choice. This dog finds its greatest happiness in following your commands, and it is in doing challenging work that herding dogs find fulfillment. If you're an authoritative person who can supply plenty of intellectually stimulating work (it needn't be actual herding; Frisbee catching and agility courses fit the bill perfectly), then you'll have a contented pet for life. If not, this dog will probably take the matter into its own hands by herding you, the family, or—an unhappy scenario—cars, bikes, and Rollerbladers. Herding dogs just have to herd.

The Working Group

Working dogs also are dogs that are happiest doing meaningful work. Included in this group are guard dogs, police dogs, patrol dogs, guide dogs, sled dogs, and rescue dogs, among them the Alaskan Malamute, Boxer, Doberman Pinscher, Rottweiler, Akita, and Siberian Husky. Most Working Group dogs are large, powerfully built, and strong; those used for guard and patrol work are territorial and bred for aggression. All require a strong hand and early training in order to develop into the loyal companions they were born to be. Working dogs are great for a strong-minded person who can stay in control of his dog, though definitely a wrong choice for the physically fragile or elderly. They're simply too powerful. Rumor to the contrary, breeds such as Rottweilers and Akitas, when properly socialized and trained, can be the most loyal and gentle of dogs. But, like all of this group, they require an authoritative owner and even then they'll constantly challenge that authority. These dogs won't accept orders from a tentative boss. Moral here: Make sure you're up to the job!

The Terrier Group

Even to those who own and love them, terriers can be terrors. They're strong willed and scrappy, determined and courageous. Bred to root out and kill small game such as foxes and weasels, their hunting instinct produces a "go get 'em" attitude that makes terriers feisty, aggressive, and territorial. They're also fiercely loyal (though not demonstratively affectionate) and, though usually small, make terrific watch dogs. The Terrier Group includes some of our best-loved breeds: West Highland Terriers (Westies), Fox Terriers, Cairn Terriers, Wheaten Terriers, and Miniature Schnauzers. Taking on a terrier means being prepared to rule the roost with a very firm hand. If you don't, the terrier will! They need owners who are energetic, active, and authoritative and can keep in check the terrier's naturally scrappy disposition. They're independent creatures, so if you're looking for an adoring, cuddly lapdog, you probably will be disappointed. Terriers love non-stop play and they're definitely not for the faint-hearted, the unassertive, or those who aren't interested in living with a dynamo.

The Hound Group

Hounds, over the centuries, have been bred to help man hunt game. They come in two types: scent hounds, which track game by scent, baying during the pursuit to lead the hunter to the game, and sight hounds, which sight prey and then use their power and speed to run it to ground. Hounds also come in all sizes, shapes, and temperaments, from the long-and-low Dachshund to the ever-popular Beagle to the sleek, graceful, and elegant Borzoi, but anyone considering acquiring a hound should know that it's a dog with tremendous instinct for the hunt. Since this hound's driving force is his enormously capable nose, scent hounds usually keep their noses to the ground (often to the annoyance of owners), checking out and reading every intriguing smell. Sight hounds, on the other hand, are stimulated by anything that moves, whether it's game or just joggers, bikers, or running children. For sight hounds, the thrill is in the chase, and an inattentive owner could find himself being dragged down the street behind a hound chasing a squirrel. Both types of hounds were bred to work strenuously in the field and consequently all hounds need vigorous exercise—at least two hours a day. Hounds are happiest when active, no doubt about that, but if hunting's not on the agenda, a sight hound will be equally delighted with a game of catch-the-Frisbee, while a scent hound revels in hide-and-seek games. (Just watch a Dachshund root out kids from under the bedcovers to see what I mean!) Hounds are determined, friendly, dedicated to pleasing their owners, and extremely loyal. Blessed with abundant energy, they're ready to go, rain or shine. If you can keep them active, you can keep them happy, which means you will be too.

The Toy Group

Born to be cuddled, the Toy Group was bred by nobility as lap dogs. (Centuries ago, before central heating, there was a practical purpose for a tiny, warm creature in one's lap.) There are twenty-one breeds classified as Toy, including Pomeranians, Toy Poodles, Maltese, King Charles Spaniels, and Italian Greyhounds, all quite different from one another, all diminutive examples of their larger relatives, giving you a great dog in a manageable package. But don't be misled by size; toy breeds often are energy-loaded, and many view themselves as big dogs. Just watch a Chihuahua fearlessly stand down a Rottweiler (a good time for the owner to scoop up the tiny warrior!) to see what I mean. Toys are a great choice for a family that wants to have multiple pooches in minimal space. They have a long life span (15 to 21 years) and are devoted to their owners and family. Their diminutive size gives them a sense of dependence that strengthens the dog/owner bond. Toys are great doll-size dogs for kids (who must always be reminded they are *not* dolls), a perfect choice for older people since they're easily paper-trained and don't have to be walked, and an ideal choice for indefatigable travelers who want to take their pooch along for the trip. And they make the best possible dog for the first-time dog owner. After all, it's hard to be intimidated by an eight-pound pooch! If you want to keep a toy dog happy, then give it what it was born to get: attention, admiration, fondling, and love. And, of course, include it in absolutely everything you do. In return, you'll get complete devotion and a protective little watchdog to boot. They may be tiny, but they do make noise.

The Non-Sporting Group

The Non-Sporting Group was designed as a catch-all group for breeds that had outlived their original purpose—dogs such as Dalmatians, which were once coach dogs but now have no coaches to follow (though they look great on fire trucks), or Bulldogs, which, thankfully, are no longer used in the cruel sport of bull-baiting. The Non-Sporting Group includes twenty-one wonderful breeds—small dogs, big dogs, hound-type dogs, and lap dogs—and here you'll find such disparate breeds as Chow Chows, Finnish Spitz, Bichon Frises, and, surprisingly, Boston Terriers (goes to show you can't always recognize a dog by its group). So how, then, can you know whether a non-sporting dog is for you? Do your homework even more scrupulously. Since the Non-Sporting Group is highly breed-specific, read everything possible about the breed that appeals to you, noting any characteristics, such as temperament and physical attributes, that might make it unsuitable for your lifestyle. Check out whether it requires more exercise, veterinary care, or grooming care than you can commit to. Such research will put you far ahead of the game, because my next advice to all prospective dog owners is more of what you've just done: research, research, research.

More Research

Now it's up to you to get specific about the breed. If you know you want a retriever to accompany you on your hikes, then what kind of retriever? Golden? Labrador? Chesapeake Bay? Each comes with a distinctive set of traits to consider. If you believe a small dog would work best for you, then should you go for a Toy Poodle, a Shih Tzu, or something in between? The range of choice is enormous and the only way to make an intelligent decision is to learn everything possible about any breed on your list—and yes, you *should* be keeping a list, which you'll narrow to five finalists. A great place to begin is at the American Kennel Club, where you'll find a wealth of material on all breeds, including *The Complete Dog Book,* the official publication of the AKC, which contains the official standards for each and every breed (call their customer service line at 919-233-9767). It will give you quite specific information on whether a particular breed is good for apartment living or whether it needs an outdoor life, whether it's good with children, whether it sheds, and the exact amount of exercise it needs every day. A source like this can let you know right up front whether the dog you have in mind is appropriate for your lifestyle, and if you see that your breed of choice requires at least two hours of exercise each day, but you're at work from 9 to 5, then strike that breed from your list.

All-breed dog shows are an invaluable resource for examining dogs in person and owners and handlers can give you accurate information on their breeds—the exercise required, the

Surfing the Dognet

The Internet is a lode of information on dogs, from facts on breeds to where dog shows are being held. These are some of the sites you may find useful:

www.akc.org/index.html — The American Kennel Club page will tell you where and when dog shows are held, rules and requirements for entering, how to register your dog with the AKC, and other valuable information about purebred dogs.

http://pucky.uia.ac.be/ChezBietel/Breedbook/index.html — Facts on breeds which will help you make an appropriate selection.

http://selectsmart.com/ — A site that will help you find the right dog for you.

Additional sites, such as **Personalogic,** which matches your lifestyle to the right dog, are linked to my Web site at **www.pawsacrossamerica.com.** I'll be adding new Web sites on a regular basis, as they become available.

general temperament, whether the breed is a good choice for small children, even whether shedding is a problem.

There are countless dog publications, such as *Dog Fancy* and *Dog World,* which will give you an overview of many breeds as well as listings of breeders who have them for sale. The Internet also is a fascinating source of material, with sites that match you and your lifestyle to just the right dog. Finding a good match makes the difference between a happy, long-lived relationship and a relationship rife with problems. Internet bulletin boards may elicit important information. If, for instance, you find that most of the messages mention problem barking, you might want to rethink your choice of breeds.

A client of mine told me about a middle-aged couple who, after years of living with paper-trained Toy Poodles, decided to buy a Norwegian Elkhound. Clearly they hadn't done their homework, since they had neither the time nor the inclination to walk the dog. Soon, their expensively decorated home was destroyed, right down to the last crystal goblet, by a dog who refused to be contained behind a gate in the kitchen. And it shouldn't have been asked of him. The couple finally gave the dog up to another owner, where it's living out its very happy life on a 100-acre farm. This is a perfect example of what can occur when you forget to research the breed.

It's always best to let your head, not your heart, make the decisions. But sometimes you just can't help it; you fall in love, and when passion enters the picture, usually reason exits the scene. One of my clients fell head over heels for a Neapolitan Mastiff puppy, totally ignoring the fact that she lives in a tiny apartment with no outdoor space. Of course, she didn't bother to find out that this breed needs an inordinate amount of exercise and, powerful as it is, a very strong hand. Soon her dog was dragging this hundred-pound woman along at the end of its leash. Fortunately, she called me and we worked with the dog until it became a quiet, well-behaved pet. Of course it still needs the exercise, so the owner is getting hers as well.

Training works miracles, yes, but it's still best to think before you choose. While almost any dog can be trained and socialized (barring mental or medical aberrations), it's always easier to begin a dog/owner relationship with a dog whose DNA already has programmed it to lead your kind of life. When friends of mine lost their beloved Cocker Spaniel, they knew that no other spaniel could possibly replace Susie, so they decided to try an entirely different breed, one they could never compare to their much-loved Cocker. They chose a Cairn Terrier, expecting the same relationship they'd had with Susie, and were crestfallen when the terrier proved to be aloof, undemonstrative, and, to hear them tell it, not at all loving. That wasn't the case, of course. The terrier was just being a terrier, and genetics are one thing that even the most careful training can't change.

However, whether the choice is made with the head or the heart, getting a dog is *always* the right move and I'll do my best to help you accommodate your passion. Owning a dog is a unique experience, the one relationship in which you'll be loved unconditionally, just for being yourself. You'll discover facets of yourself you never knew, you'll develop an entirely different outlook on your life, and you'll enter into that special world where you and another creature, one from a quite different species, develop a closeness impossible in the world of human relationships. I'm willing to bet it's an experience that will transform your life.

Now let's get down to the business of selecting a breed by doing even more breed-specific research. There are countless encyclopedias on dog breeds and books specific to each breed that can give you the information you need to make an intelligent choice, preferably with your head, not your heart. Unfortunately, it's easy to fall *out* of love if your personality and your partner's are totally out of synch. And there's no place here for divorces!

Chapter 4

Picking a Purebred Pup

If you decide to buy a purebred, you're opening the door to an extraordinary new world—the world of championship dogs and the extended family of enthusiasts who devote their lives to raising, loving, and caring for the best of them. And you'll meet professional breeders, those people who can match you up with your canine soul mate, then hold your hand through the entire getting-acquainted process.

I always recommend buying from professional breeders, simply because they offer a reliable source of first-rate dogs. Yes, those adorable little puppies you see in pet shop windows are tempting, and it's all too easy to fall in love with a cute face, then walk in and walk away with a dog you know very little about. In some cases, the outcome is a happy one; in others, it isn't. That's because many pet shops buy their stock from "puppy mills"—breeding factories run by unscrupulous people more interested in a quick buck than a good dog. Many of these dogs will have serious genetic flaws that are undetectable at first, but which surface months later, when it's too late to return the dog. Not all pet shops have defective pups, of course, but it's difficult to know which are selling puppy mill animals. And while pet shop dogs come with papers (American Kennel

Club registry), many grow up to bear little resemblance to the breed they supposedly represent. Which isn't to say they aren't lovable. I have a client who bought a pet shop puppy, took it home, and has lived happily with it ever after. As she explained, "I know he's not the best of his kind, but I couldn't bear to leave him in that cage." I have to admire her for that.

At the same time, I'd prefer that you get the dog you really want—the very best of its kind—and that's exactly what you *will* get when you buy from a reputable, responsible breeder. Here, there'll be no guesswork; you'll know up front the quality of the dog you're buying, and in the unlikely event something does go wrong, any breeder worthy of his reputation will let you return the dog and will refund your money. And that money may be substantial. A pedigreed pup can cost anywhere from several hundred to several thousand dollars, and that purchase price is just a small percentage of what you'll spend on your dog over its lifetime. When you're making such a substantial investment, buying from a breeder is great insurance.

Today's breeders are absolutely passionate about their breed of choice and they work diligently and incessantly (seven-day weeks and farmers' hours, as a rule) to improve their breeds. Because of their dedication and careful breeding techniques, many genetic problems such as hip dysplasia (common to the larger breeds such as Akitas and German Shepherds) are being bred out of the dogs. Good breeders are dedicated to producing the best possible dogs, grooming them into champions, and placing them in good homes with responsible and responsive owners. The welfare of their dogs is the first order of business for professional breeders and you can be sure that they'll want to know absolutely everything about you before they'll even think of selling you one of their future-champion pups. However, once you've been accepted as an A-OK prospective owner, the breeder will become your most trusted friend and mentor and "nanny" to your dog. Most breeders believe it's their duty to educate new dog owners to the fine points of their breeds and once you've joined their extended family, you'll find it a warmly supportive world. That's why it's so important to find the right breeder, the one who'll lead you to the right dog for you, then stick by you and your four-footed pal for life.

Finding a Breeder

How do you find just the right breeder? The usual way: careful research. Once again, the best place to begin is at the American Kennel Club, where you'll find data on every AKC-recognized breed, including membership rosters of breed clubs. Contact the club of your chosen breed and ask for information on finding breeders in your area. You'll be assured of finding a reputable breeder who's serious about producing quality dogs. Pet publications such as *Dog Fancy* and *Dog World,* as well as certain consumer publications such as *Town & Country,* routinely run advertisements for purebreds, usually displaying photographs of the kennel's championship stock. If you're connected to the Internet, you'll find a world of information on hundreds of breeders, including photographs of their dogs. The advantage here is that you can e-mail any breeder and receive an immediate response. Usually the most foolproof way is word of mouth and personal recommendation. If you know someone whose dog you admire, then ask that person to recommend his or her breeder. A satisfied client is the best recommendation of all.

An Inexpensive Way to Find a Purebred Dog

An inexpensive way to acquire a purebred dog is through breed-specific rescue groups. Almost every breed has such a rescue group, which usually is associated with the national breed club and works closely with shelters to find homes for purebred dogs who've lost theirs. The American Kennel Club, 919-233-9767, can provide you with the address and telephone for the breed club of your choice; their offices, in turn, will put you in touch with that breed's rescue group. You'll read more about rescue groups on pages 105–6.

Making Contact

Once you've established a list of potential breeders, begin contacting those in your community. I believe it's always best to work close to home simply because it allows you greater access to the dogs themselves and easier communication with the breeder after you've purchased your dog. It's a good idea to take in local dog shows, particularly those put on by the club of the breed you've chosen. These shows offer wonderful opportunities for you to see the dogs, up-close and personal, and to meet the breeders who can supply you with the dog of your dreams. You'll find that professional breeders love to talk about their dogs. Take advantage of that. Tell them what you're looking for, then listen carefully to what they have to say. They'll answer any questions you may have on temperament, on inherent breed problems, on grooming care. Explain your lifestyle to them—whether you're married or single, whether you work or are home all day, whether there are kids in the family, and whether you live in the city or the country. This will let the breeder appraise your situation realistically, and the results might surprise you. In fact, you might just learn that the dog you thought you wanted would be an absolutely terrible choice for the life you lead. But one thing the breeders can do: suggest the perfect alternative and tell you where to find it. Any respectable breeder has a vested interest in placing his dog in an appropriate home, a home where the dog will get the attention, exercise, grooming care, and devotion it needs. You'd be surprised at how these needs differ from breed to breed, and no one understands that better than the breeder.

Once you've lined up the breeder with the dogs that most appeal to you, be prepared to make some choices and to undergo a rigid interview process. Both will serve you well in the long run. You'll be asked at the outset whether you want a show-quality or pet-quality dog. The reason for that is that many breeders are interested in preserving their championship lines. If you don't plan to show your dog, the line stops there. They may say they're not interested in selling for pet purposes. Please don't feel rejected. This isn't personal, it's the breeder's profession, the business in which he has invested years of work, and the choice is his to make. On the other hand, you should ask him to refer you to another breeder with quality dogs. Occasionally, a show-dogs-only breeder may have a pup that, by a quirk of fate, isn't show quality. It happens in the best of kennels and in no way impacts the quality or reputation of the kennel. Even two top champion dogs may produce a litter that just isn't up to the show ring—the bite, say, isn't up to the breed's standards, or the nose shows a bit of pigmentation where the standards permit none, or perhaps the runt of the litter is a bit too small to make the championship grade. In cases like this, even the most show-oriented breeder will be willing to sell his dog as a pet. It doesn't hurt to ask and you may wind up with a very good dog indeed.

Internet Info on Breeders

These Web sites will give you additional information on finding a breeder, as well as information about purebred dogs:

http://puppynet.com/index.html

www.netpets.com/

All are linked to my own site: **www.pawsacrossamerica.com**

To Show or Not to Show

But before you say you want just a pet, consider the wonderful world awaiting you if you decide to show your dog. I have clients who were interested only in having a loyal canine companion and afterwards became so proud of the beautiful dog they owned that they decided to go into the ring themselves. Some actually showed their dogs; others hired handlers. It's a thrilling experience to see your canine kid walk away with a blue ribbon, and it opens up an ever-widening social network for both you *and* your dog. Dogs love the attention and applause given to them during their wins. Watch them sometime—you can almost see them begging for the prize, saying, "Here I am, judge. Pick me, 'cause I'm the best!" And when they win, they literally jump for joy. I've heard people say that the show circuit is hard on the dogs, but I believe just the opposite. Dogs love the attention they get, the grooming, the primping, the petting, the "oohs" and "aahs" that come from admiring fans. Besides, meeting your dog's littermates on the show circuit makes for a fun "family reunion." You only have to watch the dogs in action to know that, for them, this stuff is fun. If you do decide, right here and now, that the show life is the life for you, then I'll have more specific suggestions for you on how to pick a pup that's blue-ribbon material.

Getting Personal

Once you've decided on a specific breeder—after you've done the research, visited the shows, and talked to everyone available about your chosen breed and decided whether you want to show the dog—then you must interview, and be interviewed by, the breeder. This should be done first by phone, then in person. Many breeders won't even consider selling to someone they haven't met. Expect the breeder to interview you thoroughly and to ask questions that you may consider somewhat nosy. It's not meant that way, but each breeder is extremely concerned with the fate of his dogs and wants to be absolutely certain that you're the right owner for this breed. I have one client who was interviewed three separate times by her prospective breeder and says it was akin to the toughest job interview she'd ever had. That's good. It shows the breeder's concern and responsibility for his dogs. If a breeder is eager to sell you a dog, no questions asked, you might want to consider a different breeder.

These are some of the questions you might expect to be asked: Are you able to give the dog the time it deserves? That means time for play, time for grooming, time for exercise, and time for just plain loving. Where and how do you live? In a city apartment or a country house? If it's an apartment, will you be responsible for seeing the dog is walked four times a day? If you can't walk it yourself, will you invest in a dog walker who will? If you live in the country, is your yard fenced? If not, will you commit to fencing it? Are there children in your family? How old? (Breeders know when their breed is not especially good with children and they'll be quick to warn you away from that particular choice.) Have you ever had dogs before? What breed? Have you a dog now? What's its age? If it's an older dog, what will its response be to a puppy? (If it's a laid-back older dog, that's usually fine; an aggressive older dog means no sale!) One breeder tells me these questions often make a prospective buyer rethink the project entirely. Some people realize they really can't commit the time or the money needed to maintain the dog properly; others see that bringing a new puppy home to an old and ailing dog would be unfair and might cause injury to the puppy. Others just had no idea that bringing home a canine baby is just about as much work as bringing home a real one! Remember that the breeder's primary interest is in the future welfare of the dog.

This dual interview is as important for you as for the breeder. While his job is to place his dog in a good home, yours is to find the best dog for you, and a one-on-one meeting gives you a chance to get to know the breeder and decide whether this is a person you feel comfortable with, one you can trust. After all, when you buy a breeder's dog, you're setting up a relationship that will last as long as the dog lives. Your breeder will become your confidant, your adviser, your best friend in the dog world. It helps when you like one another.

By the way, I have no doubt that if you've done your research correctly, which means with great care, when you visit the breeder's kennel you'll find a spotless state-of-the-art facility with happy, healthy looking dogs. If you see anything less—smelly kennels, dirty cages, nervous dogs—then turn and head for the door, fast!

At your first meeting, discuss with the breeder why you want his breed of dog. Keep in mind that breeders always breed for temperament and characteristics that are specific to that particular breed. Knowing what these characteristics are will help you recognize, even in puppies, the genetic qualities that make a pup a good example of its breed. Perhaps after hearing the breeder's description of his breed, you may decide on a different breed entirely. The breed may be too high-strung for city living or too delicate for the country, or it may require more exercise than you could possibly give it. This is the time for rethinking your decision. As in marriage, it's better to change your mind at the altar than to spend a lifetime regretting it.

Picking Your *Pup*

Your breeder will let you know when a litter is due and when you can visit your puppy-to-be (usually at about six weeks). Even though you won't be allowed to take your pup home until it's at least eight weeks old and weaned (though occasionally breeders have older pups that are "ready to go"), most breeders will ask you to reserve your pup at the first visit or risk losing out. Having the entire litter together in one place offers the perfect opportunity for picking the pick of the litter.

I've designed a foolproof Five-Point Temperament Test which will assure that you choose the best of the best. The test was designed for puppies eight weeks to six months, the age at which a dog's temperament and personality are fully developed, but even if you're picking a six-month-old puppy, this test remains the best guideline for spotting any potential problems at a very early age. Before you administer the test, though, let me give you a crash course in DogSpeak (which, in just a few chapters, you'll learn from its alphabet to its grammar). Consider this a quick-reference guide to DogSpeak which will assure that the dog you choose will be a winner.

You will administer the Five-Point Temperament Test by working with the entire litter. Before you do, take a look at each puppy individually and carefully.

- **Observe His Expression.** If a pup has a lively, alert, and happy expression, chances are good that he's a happy, intelligent dog. If he looks slightly cowed, doesn't want to make eye contact, and is reluctant to interact with you, he's probably a timid, fearful pup. You'll learn even more by looking at those parts of your pup's body that communicate most eloquently in DogSpeak.

- **Watch His Ears.** Ears that lift (or prick up) at the slightest noise or motion tell you in DogSpeak that you have a very alert and aware pup. That's a plus. Ears held low and drooping (this also applies to droopy-eared dogs such as spaniels) are DogSpeak indicators of apprehension or fear and may be a signal that this is a fearful or timid pup. That would be a minus.

- **Look into His Eyes.** Just as with humans, bright, wide-open eyes are indicative of intelligence, alertness, and curiosity. If the expression in his eyes is eager, he's saying in DogSpeak, "I'd like to play with you." I can think of no nicer qualities in a dog, can you? This is a definite plus. If the pup avoids eye contact or slightly lowers his lids, that's DogSpeak for a fearful, timid disposition—a minus.

- **Check His Body Language.** An upright body posture, with head held high, ears pricked, and tail up and wagging says clearly in DogSpeak, "I'm the dog for you!" A cowering body, with tail held between the legs, ears low and drooping, and eyes averted says in DogSpeak's most powerful message, "I'm scared and I might be a problem." Since problems aren't what you're looking for, this DogSpeak message is a very big minus.

- **Listen to His Voice.** By nature, puppies whine, whimper, and yip. As any child knows, that's the best way to get mommy's attention. Sharp puppy-sized barks are natural DogSpeak communication saying "Pay attention, something's going on." But a growl says in DogSpeak, "Stay away from me. Don't come any nearer." That's a double-minus message that says this pup is potentially aggressive.

Now, with your DogSpeak phrases at the ready, it's time to administer the Five-Point Temperament Test to the entire litter of pups. As you judge each pup, keep a written record of its good and not-so-good points. This written "report card" will help you weigh the pluses and minuses of each puppy. The minuses won't go away and they won't improve as the puppy grows into adulthood. If minuses far outweigh pluses, it would be wise to choose another pup. Any reputable breeder will be delighted by your commitment to making an intelligent choice and will gladly let you put his puppies to the test. He wants both his dog and you, the owner, to be happy and, if he's a top-flight breeder, he knows his dogs can pass with flying colors. If the breeder seems annoyed that you want to give such a test, my advice is to move on to another breeder—this one must have something to hide.

The Five-Point Temperament Test

1. Carefully observe the interaction of the litter. You'll see in a flash that there are pups with either dominant or submissive personalities, the future Alphas or Omegas of your pack-to-be. The dog that bullies the others, hovering over them, pushing them away from the food and showing his position as "top pup" is, beyond any doubt, an Alpha in the making. He's saying, in loud and clear DogSpeak, "I rule the roost." You can be sure this pup will be hard to handle and rebellious, testing your authority on a daily basis. The more submissive dog that stays apart in a corner, rarely interacting and, in extreme cases, cowering and shivering in fear, is at the bottom of the litter's hierarchy, the Omega. His DogSpeak body language is telling you that he's timid, standoffish, and afraid of confrontation. He may be so panicky that he'll find it hard to focus on future training. Neither the bully nor the fearful dog is a good choice. The perfect pup is the one that interacts in a calm, alert, sociable, and playful way, taking your presence in stride.

2. Clap your hands sharply and observe the reaction of the pups to the sound. Some will look up inquisitively (the ideal response), others will run for cover (too nervous), and some will growl or bark and run towards you (overly aggressive). If the dog doesn't show any response to a clap, it's a good bet the dog is deaf. A bark could be a simple alert signal, but growling when you approach is a clear DogSpeak warning that the pup is an aggression problem you should leave with the breeder.

3. Pick up each pup, one at a time, cradle it in your arms, and see how each responds to your holding it. If the pup is quiet and relaxed, taking your handling in stride, that's a sign that he already has trust in you. A struggle against being handled may indicate either an overly dominant or overly fearful dog. Fighting your touch is the flight-or-fight response in microcosm. The fearful pup may tremble or revert to an age-old protective instinct and freeze. Any dog this nervous will prove to be problematic. A pup that growls while you hold it is far too aggressive. The perfect pup is one that's confident, relaxed, and friendly, reveling in your attention. *That's* the one to take home!

4. To test further the pup's response to handling, gently touch its ears and its toes, softly massaging its body. What you're doing is reproducing the mother's reassuring touch, her nuzzling, her licking. It's an experience most pups will love. But, once again, if the puppy shivers and whimpers (too fearful) or growls and snaps (far too aggressive), it's not a dog you want. Leave it there. Your goal is a pup that remains happy, playful, and positive, no matter what the challenge.

5. To test inquisitive behavior and alertness, toss a squeaky toy or any other noisy object into the pups' pen. If a dog is curious, picks up the object, and plays with it, that indicates he has a healthy interest in everything around him. He's alert, attentive, and playful. His ears are up, his eyes focused on this newfound object, and his body may be doing a DogSpeak play bow, the signal that says "Let's have some fun!" But if the pup runs away from the object, it indicates a nervous, fearful disposition—a drawback that doesn't improve with age. Working with each dog individually, roll the toy along the ground. If it picks up the toy and plays with it, you have a relaxed, playful pup. And if it brings it back to you, well, he's telling you in DogSpeak, "I'm a born retriever!"

If, by the way, you fall in love with a particular pup that didn't make A-grades on the test, that doesn't mean you shouldn't have it. Many faults *can* be corrected with proper training. You just may have to work at that training a bit harder. It's up to you!

Long-Distance Love

It may be that you've set your heart on a certain breed of dog only to discover that there is no breeder within hundreds of miles of where you live. What then? Do your research diligently, working with the information department of that breed's club. Ordering a dog by mail can be risky business and it's always safer (and probably more cost-effective in the long run) to travel a reasonable distance to view the pups for yourself. But if that just isn't possible, and you won't consider any other breed, then it's crucially important that you line up breeders with flawless reputations. *Check their references.* You'll be asking someone you've never met to select your lifetime canine mate. You and the breeder must ask each other some very important questions. If the breeder *doesn't* question you carefully about your circumstances—your lifestyle, who will care for the dog, how much time you can spend with it, and whether your yard (if you have one) is safely fenced—then chances are you've gotten a breeder who's too eager to sell his dogs to an unknown buyer. *Walk away and keep looking.* Right up front in the negotiation, determine the breeder's return policy on the dog. Will he return your money if, for any reason, the dog doesn't stack up to your expectations, as long as you agree to pay shipping costs? Most breeders not only will do so but will insist on getting the dog back if you're unhappy. Then *ask for a written contract* to protect both you and the breeder.

Get It in Writing

Whether you buy in person or take the risk of getting your dog from a breeder you've never met, my advice is always the same: Sign a contract. It will save a great deal of trouble if something should go wrong down the line. The contract should spell out clearly that if you get the dog and decide you don't want it or for any reason just can't keep it, the breeder will accept its return. At the same time, it will assure the breeder that you won't place the dog with anyone else, even members of your immediate family. Good breeders always want to control the fate of their dogs and any reputable breeder will return your money, asking only that you pay shipping. As an extra protection, ask the breeder for a veterinarian certificate showing that the dog has been x-rayed and does not have hip dysplasia (this is especially important for large breeds with a genetic tendency to the problem). If you get a dog with serious defects such as epilepsy or hip dysplasia, even when those problems don't show up for a period of time, the breeder still should be willing to take the dog back and return your money. (The problem here is that later you may not be able to part with your beloved dog.)

If, on the other hand, the dog arrives looking sick, take it to a veterinarian *at once* to determine the problem. If it's been shipped, perhaps it's a touch jet-lagged, nothing serious. But if a real medical problem shows up, telephone the breeder and, in your most diplomatic way, say, "I'm sure you didn't know this, but this is a very sick dog." More likely than not, the breeder didn't knowingly sell you a sick dog and will want you to return it promptly. If you've done your research properly, you'll be working with a scrupulously honest professional, one who will become your confidant, mentor, and best dog buddy. That's why it's important to know as much as possible about the breeder you've chosen. *Caveat emptor.*

Chapter 5

The Homecoming

I'm always amazed when I hear about people who buy puppies and bring them home without having made the slightest preparation. You wouldn't bring a baby home from the hospital without first providing a crib, would you? You certainly would be sure you had your pediatrician already lined up. You'd have a good supply of formula, bottles, and diapers, and I feel reasonably sure you'd have picked out a name. Well, I hope you'll do the same for your pup. After all, this is your newly adopted four-legged child and it's coming home to a new environment. Just imagine how it feels, taken away from its mother and siblings, going to a strange place and leaving all its security behind. It's an unnerving experience for a pup. It's your job as the new parent/owner to take over its real mother's job as comforter, protector, teacher, and unquestioned authority. Doing so gives you a wonderful opportunity to guide this tiny puppy through the beginning of its life so that, just as with real kids, it will grow up to be a balanced, happy, healthy dog. Even more important, it provides crucially important bonding between you and your dog.

The Dog Owner's Starter Kit

There are many things you can do to ease your pup's transition from its home to yours, not the least of which is having everything ready *before* you bring it home. There are nine essential tools you'll need to have in place before you pick up your pup:

- Collar
- Leash
- Crate or airline kennel cab
- Bowls for food and water
- Food
- Pressure gate or expandable playpen
- The "BashRoom," an indoor bathroom tray and "piddle pads"
- Brush and comb
- Toys and chews

The Collar

Sounds easy, doesn't it? Just pop in your local pet shop and pop out with a beautiful collar. But getting the *right* collar is supremely important to training your pup. Many people buy a too-large collar, expecting the puppy to grow into it. This can let the pup slip out of its collar—a dangerous situation indeed—and will make it much more difficult to correct the puppy during training. So it's important to get the correct collar at once, in the correct size.

Chain-link collars are, in my opinion, the essential training tool. These collars are made up of metal chain links with a ring at each end which tightens or releases the collar at the owner's tug. Used correctly, this tighten/release mechanism sends an immediate and clear message to the dog about its behavior: If it pulls, the collar will tighten; when it stops pulling and walks calmly, the collar loosens comfortably. I call such collars "control collars." Some people view control collars negatively, believing (wrongly) that their use is a cruel way to correct and control a dog. Nothing could be further from the truth. The control collar, correctly fitted, is the best possible take-charge tool and the quintessential training aid. Dogs trained with these are perfectly happy—and perfectly behaved, once they've learned to respond to its tighten/release signals. Of course, it's up to you, the Alpha/owner, to use the collar correctly, and of course I'll give you specific instructions on that, when we begin training your dog.

Very young or very small puppies are too fragile to be fitted out with the traditional chain-link control collars. For small pups, I recommend a soft leather or nylon buckle collar or a show lead (a combination of collar and leash). A buckle collar should be snug but not tight. Buy a size that fits snugly enough so that it won't slip off over the pup's head, but still has plenty of expansion room to accommodate your pup's always rapid growth. A perfect fit lets you slip two fingers between the collar and the pup's throat. If you can't, it's too tight. And since your pup will grow practically before your eyes, *always* keep a sharp eye out for a collar that's getting too tight.

At about three to five months old, a pup can graduate to a nylon control collar, or slip collar. This works exactly like the traditional chain control collar, tightening and releasing as the owner pulls or loosens the leash. Larger breeds, such as Pit Bulls, Rottweilers, and Labradors, obviously need greater control, and by four to six months of age should be fitted with a chain control collar.

Chain-link control collars come in a variety of styles, and there are even vinyl-coated "fur-saver" collars with larger links for long-haired breeds. The rule of thumb for a correct fitting: The collar should slip easily, but not loosely, over the dog's head. When pulled snug, there should be a couple of inches of chain extension, allowing room for the release action. Since some dogs have large heads in relation to their necks and others, such as Scottish Deer Hounds, have small ones, the excess chain may vary in length. Your local pet-supply shop can help you find the perfect fit for your dog.

Putting on the control collar often seems an exercise in futility for novice dog owners. It looks a bit like a Chinese puzzle, and how on earth can anyone put one big ring through another of the same size? You don't! Holding one ring in your left hand and the other in your right, feed the *chain* down through the right-hand ring, as if you were threading a needle. Then hold the collar up in the shape of a "P." There's your training collar! Slip it over the dog's head, making sure the excess chain, or tail of the "P," hangs to the *right side* of your dog's neck. (You'll always work with the dog to your left side.) The chain should slide easily up and down as you pull or release the leash. If it doesn't, but locks in place when you tug the leash, chances are you've made a "Q" instead of a "P" and put the collar on backwards. Remove the collar, turn it around, and try again. The secret of the control collar's success lies in the tighten/release motion, achieved by the chain's sliding smoothly in and out of the ring. Practice until you're sure you have your dog's collar working properly. Otherwise, the dog will feel choked and you'll get no response from your commands.

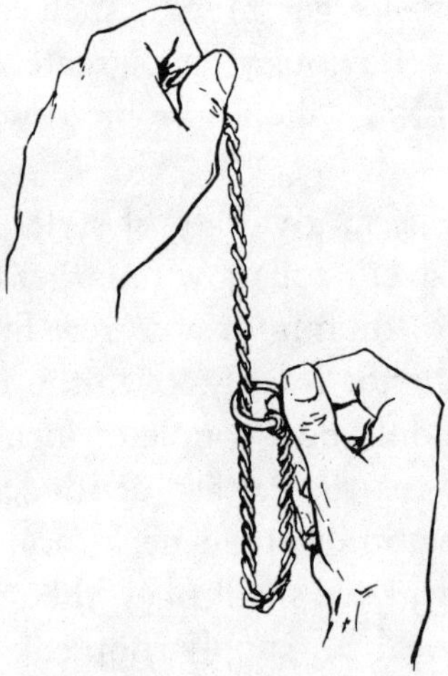

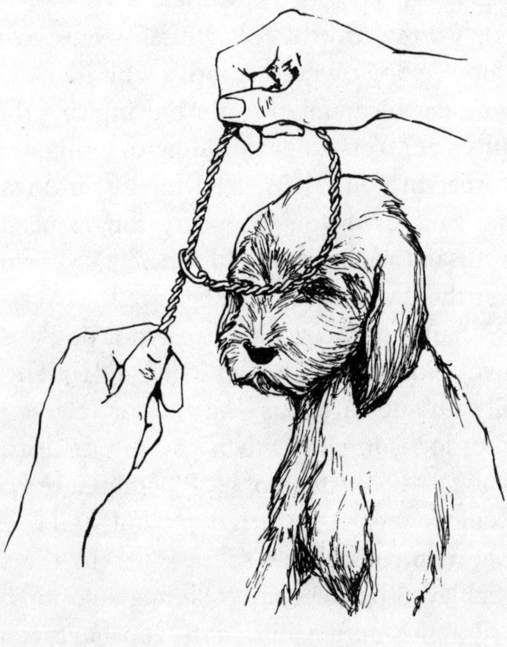

To use the control collar, thread the chain down through the ring, to form a "P."

The Leash

I always advise getting a six-foot leash, which can be either nylon or leather. Both are durable; the advantage of nylon is that it's also washable. Choose a leash that's comfortable in your hand. (Chain link isn't, which is why I never recommend a metal leash.) The six-foot length gives you the option of holding the dog close, for on-leash control, or giving the dog six feet of separation when it needs to relieve itself. (A perfectly obedient dog actually will relieve itself on the owner's command, in the spot the owner indicates.) A six-foot leash also is useful for training the dog to walk off-leash since when the leash is draped around the owner's neck it gives the dog the illusion that it's heeling off-leash. Remember, the leash is your connection to your dog and your tool for anticipating your dog's every move.

The Crate or Kennel

Next to collar and leash, the crate is perhaps the single most important tool of dog training. It's essential for housebreaking, crucial to solving problems such as separation anxiety, a solution for destructive behavior, a prevention for unacceptable behavior, and, as if that weren't enough, a wonderful safe haven for your dog. I've heard those who don't know better say, "I wouldn't put my dog in a cage!" They certainly aren't taking the dog's wishes into consideration. Every dog needs a place of its own. Every dog needs a place where it can be confined for its own safety. Every dog needs a place where it can learn the parameters of good canine behavior. The crate answers all three requirements, and if you check out those dogs who've been accustomed to a crate, you'll find that, more often than not, the dog considers the crate its "room," a place where it can get away from the often intimidating world outside, where it can relax, secure in the knowledge that it won't be disturbed. In effect, the crate becomes a dog's own private den, and since den behavior is one of the Eight Central Factors of Pack Behavior that is very much alive in all domestic dogs, a den is requisite to having a happy dog. You certainly wouldn't put a newborn baby to sleep in an adult's bed, or put it on the floor to play without the safety and security of a playpen. That's an invitation to disaster. Both babies and puppies need to be in a protective environment, so please think of your dog's crate as its crib, playpen, and wolf-pup den rolled into one. It's the only way to keep your pup, and your household, under control.

There are two types of crates: the traditional wire crate, which looks much like a cage, and the kennel cab, the carrier used by airlines. Personally, I prefer the traditional wire crate because it gives the dog a 360-degree view of the outside world, letting him remain in visual contact with his family while he's safe and secure within his den. When the dog needs quiet—say, if he's recuperating from surgery—a blanket draped over the crate creates a totally private, quiet space. Kennel cabs, on the other hand, being more enclosed and giving the dog less visual stimuli, may give a nervous dog additional security and comfort (the very reason these are used for plane travel). And for a large, powerful dog who's an accomplished escape artist, the fully enclosed kennel cab is practically escape-proof.

Whether you choose a crate or a kennel cab, it's important to buy the right size. A grown dog should be able to turn around and lie down comfortably inside the crate or carrier, yet it shouldn't be overly roomy, particularly if it's meant for travel. If a travel carrier is too large, the dog might be tossed about in-transit. Wire crates are extremely versatile and can be fitted out with dividers to enlarge or shrink their inner dimensions. Some styles are collapsible for easy moving and/or storage; others are made with side doors to function within station wagons or vans. I always recommend buying the size crate your dog will need when it reaches adulthood. You always can reduce the crate's size to fit a pup. This maintains a micro-environment, leaving less free space for potential bathroom mistakes and providing additional security for small puppies, who really want to feel snug and secure in a small space—just like their ancestral den. Reducing the size of a molded-plastic kennel cab is not so simple, so if you're planning to use one for actual travel, please buy the proper fit for the dog *at the time of the trip,* then replace it with a bigger size as the dog grows. Better to be safe than very, very sorry. Any pet-supply shop will guide you in choosing the correct size.

By the way, both crate and kennel cab should be cushioned with comfortable padding. There are pads made to fit all crates, or you can make your own mattress out of towels or a pillow. After all, cold steel or bumpy molded plastic are *not* comfortable places for a dog to sleep.

Bowls for Food and Water

One of my clients feeds her dog out of a priceless antique porcelain bowl. To each his own! I recommend stainless steel food and water bowls, simply because they are indestructible and easy to clean. These are available in all pet-supply shops and often come as a set with their own stand, which lifts them slightly off the floor. That's a good idea, not only for keeping the floors clean, but for making the food stationary and more accessible to the dog. Large breeds in particular need their food elevated, so for them bowls in stands some eight inches or so from the ground are preferred. This prevents the dog's having to stoop to eat, a position which can damage the neck and spine area. An important caution: Your dog's food and water bowls need to be kept as clean as you'd want your own to be, and water should be replenished on a regular basis, especially during hot weather. (In blistering heat, ice cubes are a great way to quench thirst and cool the dog's body temperature quickly.) It's important to keep an eye on the supply since you are your dog's only water source. If you don't, you can't blame your dog for drinking from the toilet.

Safety Alert

Word of warning: *Never* use chemicals in the toilet when there's a dog in the house. One day he might decide to test those waters, with tragic results. *Chemicals designed to freshen the toilet bowl (and that includes fresheners used in the tank) can poison your dog!*

Food

Getting the right food is the key to keeping your dog healthy. Your breeder undoubtedly has started your pup on a good regimen and is the best person to recommend a brand, since puppies' digestive systems are delicate and don't take kindly to abrupt change of diet. It's always best to keep your puppy on its current diet unless your veterinarian says otherwise. He, ultimately, is the person who will select the best diet, and the correct feeding portions, for your dog.

Now, more than ever, there is a wide variety of dog foods available, from premium quality to supermarket brands. There are even special diets for dogs with medical problems such as diabetes, kidney disorders, food allergies, and even cancer. Such a vast selection makes the choice difficult, which is why the best person to prescribe the proper diet for your dog is your veterinarian. That diet will change through the years as the dog matures and its body changes. As a rule, puppies need high-protein puppy food, though if your dog is a large-boned breed (which often experience "growing pains") your vet may recommend a diet with less protein, even for a pup. For now, and until your veterinarian says otherwise, your pup should get the same puppy food with which the breeder weaned it. Let's not rock the digestive boat!

Pressure Gate or Expandable Playpen

Depending on the space you've selected as your dog's, you'll need either a pressure gate or expandable playpen for confining it to its predetermined space. If you plan on sectioning off a small room such as a pantry or extra bathroom, a pressure gate is the answer. Pressure gates come in many styles; my preference is a wire-mesh gate with openings small enough to retain even the tiniest pup. If your pup is going to share the kitchen with you, then you need an expandable playpen to confine him in his corner of the room. Again, choose one with mesh small enough to prevent the escape of even a very small puppy.

The "BashRoom"

The "BashRoom" is the perfect housebreaking tool for puppies and small dogs. It consists of a box-framed tray that holds "piddle pads" (special pads infused with a scent that stimulates pups to urinate) or newspaper. The dog is taught to relieve itself in the BashRoom, making it a veritable litter-box for dogs.

Your local pet-supply shop will have these, or you can make your own by building a wooden frame, 18 by 24 inches and approximately two inches high, and filling it with a layer of waterproof plastic topped by a piddle pad or newspaper.

The "BashRoom," an indoor training tool.

Brush and Comb

Sounds simple, but there is an enormous range of brushes and combs available, each suitable for a different type of coat. It's important to get the right one for your dog, and your breeder should be able to recommend the appropriate choice. I suggest checking with your local grooming shop as well. Grooming on a regular basis from an early age (usually around six months, when your pup has had its final shots) is not only healthy but also encourages good social behavior in your dog. So whether you use a professional groomer or do the job yourself (I'll give you some tips later on), grooming should be a priority in your dog's life. A clean, comfortable dog is a contented dog.

Toys and Chews

Puppies, particularly when teething, exhibit the exploratory behavior of their wolf ancestors. They like to carry things about in their mouths, to chew on anything they can find. And unless you want your pup chewing on your sofa or your best pair of shoes, it's wise to provide it with its own chewable goodies. However, it's important to select toys that are safe, and chews that are both safe and "chewy" enough to work off the pup's natural chewing instincts. You need to be just as careful with your pup's toys as you would with your baby's, so don't choose anything small enough to be swallowed. For safety's sake, consult your veterinarian on appropriate toys and chews and, obviously, keep an eye on your pup. If he tears apart a toy, he may swallow its parts. *Take that toy away* and replace it with something sturdier.

Tool Chest

All of the tools in the Dog Owner's Starter Kit are available at pet-supply shops; most are also available through pet catalogs or on the Internet, where there's a growing group of dog-related Web sites, including my own site at www.pawsacrossamerica.com.

Some helpful catalogs are:

J & B Wholesale Pet Supplies, Inc. (800-526-0388)

Drs. Foster & Smith Pet Products & Supplies (800-562-7169)

Cherrybrook Pet Products (800-524-0820)

R. C. Steel (800-872-4506)

(continues on next page)

(continued)

Additional Web sites are:

www.netpets.com

www.acmepet.com/market/index/html

www.acmepet.com/market/index/html

www.petquarters.com/cgu-bin/petquarters.storefront

www.aardvarkpet.com

www.jbpet.com

www.cherrybrook.com

Other Necessities

The Dog Owner's Starter Kit is just that—a starting point. But before you bring your puppy into your home, you also should have planned the following in advance:

- A space of its own
- A veterinarian
- A name

The Puppy's "Room"

Before you bring this new family member home, pick out the place that will become "the puppy's room," the most convenient place in the house to confine it. And yes, "confine" is exactly what I mean. Giving a small puppy the run of the house is the *wrong* thing to do and would be overwhelming for it. At this tender age, a puppy needs a simple, small, secure environment where it feels completely safe. That space will become its "room," where it will begin to learn the elements of canine good behavior, including housebreaking. I call this "micro-training" since it reduces the pup's world to the simplest, most basic elements.

A good rule of thumb is a space no more than double the size of the crate or kennel, whichever you've selected to serve as the puppy's sleeping place, or den. Within that small space, there should be room for the crate, food and water bowls, an indoor bathroom tray, and toys. Even at a tender age, puppies try not to relieve themselves where they sleep or eat. By keeping the space tight, you give the pup little choice but to sleep in his crate, use the BashRoom or piddle pad to relieve himself, and reserve a space for play. This micro-environment reduces the opportunities for bathroom mistakes and will make the entire housebreaking process easier. Later on, when your pup feels entirely in control of his micro-environment, he can graduate to the macro-environment of the great big world outside. *Then* he can have the run of the house and you'll never have to worry—he'll already have learned the parameters. For now, always remember that young puppies just aren't capable of making wise choices. It's up to you, the owner, to do that for them.

Where and How

I always suggest setting up the puppy's room in an area such as an extra bathroom, an unused foyer, or a portion of the kitchen. It's best to avoid carpeted rooms since, to a pup, carpets are just oversized piddle pads. Try to pick a room with easily cleaned tile floors, since even piddle pads aren't 100 percent waterproof! If you have only wood floors or wall-to-wall carpets, then at least protect those by covering the pup's area with a plastic tarpaulin or drop cloth.

The pup can be confined in one of two ways: with a pressure gate, used to close off the space, or with a portable "playpen." Both are available at pet-supply stores, and both are effective barriers. Within the area you've enclosed as your pup's space, place the crate or carrier that will serve as its den and sleeping quarters, food and water bowls, toys, papers to protect the floor (it's always easier to toss out papers than mop the floors), and your BashRoom, the indispensable housebreaking tool. This space is where your puppy will spend its babyhood—its "childhood room," so to speak—and where it will learn how to adapt to a strict schedule of eating, sleeping, and relieving itself that will keep everyone in the household—the puppy included—happy.

Lining Up a Veterinarian

How to find a competent veterinarian? The usual way: research, research, research. The best possible recommendation for a veterinarian, of course, is a satisfied client, so begin by asking your dog-owner friends what vet they use. You might want to ask, as well, about the doctor's rates, his office hours, and his location. All are important when your dog is sick, and even the most brilliant vet will be of no help in an emergency if he's fifty miles away. If you don't know anyone with a dog, contact your local Veterinary Society and ask for a list of veterinarians in your community. All vets are qualified; some are more specialized, with board certification in areas such as ophthalmology, surgery, or dermatology. You don't need those yet, but you do need a reliable all-around vet.

Once you've compiled a list of the most likely candidates,

make appointments to interview every vet on the list. The client/veterinarian relationship is one of the most important on earth and your vet not only must be a competent, experienced medical professional, but also should have a kind and gentle manner with your pet. Since you won't have your pet with you for the first interview, you'll have to make a judgment based on the vet's interaction with you. Remember: This is a relationship that will last for the life of your dog. It's supremely important that there be empathy. If for some reason your personalities just don't mesh, interview another veterinarian. Yes, skill is the most important requisite, but compassion and kindness are large parts of the equation.

Once you've decided on a veterinarian, make an appointment for him to see your pup no more than two days after you've brought the puppy home. (Obviously, if the dog seems sick, take it to the doctor immediately!) The pup will need a thorough going-over to be sure he's healthy, and he'll need his first inoculations, to protect him against distemper, hepatitis, and leptosporosis. Your vet will tell you that young puppies need to be isolated from other dogs until the final shots, usually given at about three or four months. This is to protect your pup against parasites and diseases. Even after he's had his final shots, you should avoid letting the puppy sniff fresh urine or feces, both of which can contain parasites that might infect your dog.

Naming the New "Baby"

Now for a name. You met your puppy a couple of weeks ago, so you probably already have a sense of its personality. It will speed the training process greatly if you can call the pup by its *real* name from the moment it leaves the kennel. There are scores of baby-name books that will help you make a choice. I have some advice as well: Dogs respond best to short, snappy words with sharp consonants—Fritz, Spot, Duke, King, Inger, Sally, and Sara are good examples. *Don't* give a dog anything as complicated as "Abigail," "Horatio," or "Beauregard." Why not? Because when dogs communicate with each other in their own language, they do so with yips and barks—short, sharp sounds. That's DogSpeak, and giving your pup a proper DogSpeak name will make communicating with it all the easier.

Off to Pick Up the Puppy

Naturally, everyone wants to go along to bring the puppy home. But it's always a wise idea to ask the breeder whether that's all right, since some breeders may feel that so much excitement would overwhelm the pup. If that's the case, leave the kids at home and make it their responsibility to have the puppy's room prepared and ready. Remind them they'll have plenty of time for play, for years to come. If two of you are going to pick up the dog, one should take along a couple of towels for holding the pup. This is a new baby, remember, and it probably will wet en route. Please don't just dump a puppy in the back seat! It's not only dangerous but would terrify the pup. Hold it, caress it, reassure it. It needs your love and your care. If you're traveling alone, and you're picking up a small breed, then take along a dog carrier. If the dog is larger, take along a crate. Both are readily available at pet-supply shops. As a carrier, I recommend the Sherpa bag, which is soft and cushioned. Might as well buy the size that will accommodate your dog when it's grown since you'll undoubtedly be taking future trips and there's no point in having to buy another later.

If you're faced with a long trip of more than thirty minutes, also take along a doggie baby bottle filled with water (pet shops sell these). When there are two of you, one can give the puppy its water bottle while in transit. If you're traveling alone, you'll need to make a rest stop to water the puppy. Remember: Be sensible about giving water—just enough to wet the puppy's mouth, but not enough to make it throw up. Puppies have delicate tummies.

You're Home!

And of course, all the family wants to greet the puppy. *Tender* greetings are fine, and every member of the family should be able to experience holding and caressing the puppy. But keep in mind that the pup has just been through a very traumatic experience. Please don't overwhelm it with affection. Remember that polite question once asked of arriving guests: "Would you like to refresh yourself?" Do the same for your puppy. Let it have a place to relieve itself, either on the paper or the piddle pads you've already put down, or, if you have a fenced backyard safe from other dogs, on the grass. It's a good idea to accustom a puppy at once to the experience of the leash. Even if you plan to paper-train it, slip the leash on and let it grow accustomed to walking about its designated space dragging the leash. If you're taking it outdoors, slip the leash and collar on the puppy, then walk gently along beside the puppy. You shouldn't feel any pressure on the leash (in other words, *don't* drag the pup), but the puppy will know that it's attached to you by this leash and eventually will view walking on-leash as the norm. Once outdoors, give your puppy a chance to get its bearings, to sniff out this new, strange place and to assimilate all the new smells, sounds, and voices that are surrounding it. When it urinates, it will be marking your home as its own. That's Dog-

Speak for, "This is *my* place," and it gives a pup a wonderful feeling of security to know he has a safe haven.

The pup probably will be hungry—after all, he hasn't eaten since he left the kennel—and he's probably ready for a nap, since the whole experience has been exhausting. The most important thing, right now, is not to traumatize him with too much handling. There's plenty of time for that later, when he wakes up! Puppies, as I will continue to remind you, really are much like babies. They need plenty of sleep, regular feedings, and constant changing (not of diapers, but of piddle pads or paper). Keeping in mind that this really is a tiny new creature, just starting its life, will help you maintain the perspective needed to see you through the period of adjustment just ahead.

The most important thing you can do to ensure your puppy's health, good habits, and training in the future is to begin *now* to establish a reliable schedule. That includes feeding time, bathroom time, play time, and training time. It will make your own life far simpler down the road if the dog understands exactly when he will eat, when he *must* relieve himself, and when you both can relax with a nice game of ball. I can't emphasize strongly enough the importance of establishing this schedule *immediately,* then being committed to following that schedule throughout the life of your dog. Imagine how you would feel if you could never be sure when (or if) you might eat or when you'd be able to use the bathroom. I think most humans would develop serious nervous problems very quickly indeed! Dogs are remarkably forgiving, but forgetting to feed, water, or walk your dog is, in my book, an unforgivable sin.

Housebreaking Begins

You probably decided before you got the pup whether you wanted it paper-trained or completely housebroken. Much of that decision depends on your lifestyle and, of course, whether the dog is large or small. Large dogs really do have to be walked and it would be cruel to try to paper-train one. Besides, large dogs need a proportionate amount of exercise. With a small dog, the choice really is yours: Some people hate having to walk the dog, others hate the idea of picking up dirty papers. Personally, I think there's great benefit in walking your dog. It keeps you both physically fit, gives both of you a chance to socialize with other dogs and their owners, and helps reinforce the bond between you and your dog. Of course, in some cases, committing to regular walks just isn't feasible. People who have physical problems, people who are elderly and fragile, mothers with infants, or even those whose jobs keep them working long hours just can't do regular walks. With them, paper-training is the only option. But if you absolutely can't walk your dog, and can't find anyone else to walk it for you, at least select a dog small enough to be paper-trained. *Please!*

There are foolproof methods for both housebreaking and paper-training your dog. Both require commitment to a strict schedule. Puppies' bladders are small and veterinarians suggest that asking a dog to hold its urine longer than six hours may be taking a chance with its health. Kidney damage could result. However, most dogs can sleep through an eight-hour night. A word of caution: *Don't give unlimited water before bedtime* unless you don't mind getting up in the middle of the night.

The Paper-Trained Dog

Let's begin our housebreaking with the dog who will learn to use a designated spot indoors as its bathroom. The beautiful part of micro-training (keeping the pup's environment small) is that it makes crystal clear, even to a puppy, which space is for what purpose. People who give small puppies too large a space are asking for problems. That's why I always ask my clients to keep the space tight, using the double-the-crate measurement as the best possible guideline. After all, what's right for a Chihuahua is impossible for a Mastiff!

Create a quiet, comfortable bathroom space for the dog near (but not too near) its cage. You either can cover the space with paper or use the BashRoom, my own favorite housebreaking tool. It's a convenient way to keep the piddle pads out of traffic's way and neatly positioned for your pup's use. Obviously, the pup will need to learn, from you, what the tray or paper is for. That's why each time you feed and water the puppy, you'll place it on the tray. Do your best to try to catch your dog's signals. Most dogs, even puppies, will let you know when they're about to squat; they do what I call the "poo-poo dance." Some sniff and circle, others run back and forth. Both behaviors help create the impulse for the dog to go. Each dog has its own cues and learning to recognize your dog's will be your first lesson in DogSpeak. The minute you spot the behavior that says "bathroom break," pick the puppy up and place it on the paper. Timing is supremely important here! You want the puppy to get the message that here, on the paper or the piddle pad, is where it's expected to relieve itself. The pup soon will learn that this is the *only* acceptable place for him to relieve himself.

What about when you're not there? That's the beauty of the micro-environment. Since the space is so small, there's very little place to go except the intended place, whether paper or BashRoom. And since even the smallest dogs don't want to mess near their den, chances are very good they'll go on the paper or pad. After about five days, that lesson should be down pat.

Once the pup has learned to use the paper, you can begin to expand its environment. Enlarge the enclosed space, either by moving the pressure gate to make a larger area or by enlarging the playpen. Now the pup has room for his crate, his "bathroom," and an area (*without* paper) where he can play with his toys or just rest and relax. If he's learned his lesson properly, he should automatically go to the paper area or piddle pad to relieve himself. If he doesn't, shrink the space to micro once again and repeat the process, putting the pup onto the paper each time he shows signs of a bathroom urge. And remember: Each time you feed and/or water the pup, place him on the paper or piddle pad. Within a very short time, he'll be totally paper-trained.

The Outdoor Dog

Here's a foolproof way to housebreak the outdoor dog—the one you're committed to walking at least four times per day. It's a rigorously scheduled process you're about to embark on, but one that works beautifully. This schedule is intended for puppies from eight to twelve weeks up to sixteen weeks of age. After that, the pup will graduate to a schedule less demanding of your time.

Housebreaking Schedule for the Outdoor Dog (eight weeks to sixteen weeks)

6:00 A.M. Remove the pup from its crate, where it's been enclosed all night (it's important to keep the crate doors securely fastened since you don't want a puppy with a full bladder roaming your house!), and take it for a quick trip outside to relieve itself.

Once the pup has both urinated and defecated, bring the puppy back inside, and feed and water it. *Immediately,* take it back outdoors. (You'll be surprised. It *will* need to go.) This is a good time to let the pup explore its new environment and to have a short play period with you, its new owner/parent. It's also a perfect opportunity to accustom the pup further to walking on the leash. Your puppy may resist the leash at first and simply sit down, refusing to move. Be patient and persistent. Talk to it gently and encourage it to take its first on-leash steps.

After the play/training interlude, take the pup back inside and play with it a bit more. (As you can see, having a puppy is a time-consuming prospect. If you absolutely can't take the time for another play period, put the pup back into its crate.)

9:00 A.M. First give the puppy water, then another quick outdoor walk. If you have time, play with it a bit, then put it back in its crate until noon.

Noon Outdoors once more for a bathroom break, then back inside for food and water and *immediately* back outdoors. Too many people feed and water their pups, then return the puppy to the crate. That's not good! With a full bladder, the pup will be both uncomfortable and unhappy.

3:30 P.M. Give the puppy some water, then take a quick outdoor walk, after which it's back in the crate until late afternoon.

6:00 P.M. Walk the pup outdoors to relieve itself, bring it inside for the evening's last food and water, then take it out again immediately. *Don't* feed or water your pup after this walk. It would cause unnecessary suffering if he's forced to spend the night with a full bladder or tummy. However, you can give the pup a couple of ice cubes to lick, which will quench its thirst until morning without causing discomfort.

10:30–11:00 P.M. Give the pup its last walk of the day, after which you both probably will drop off to a sound sleep!

It's crucially important not to give additional water after this final walk, unless you don't mind making a midnight run. It takes only three to four hours for food and water to work its way through a puppy's system. Since what goes in also comes out, it's important that you control your puppy's intake. There's a huge difference between control and deprivation and I can assure you that your puppy will be far more comfortable with his thirst quenched by ice but his bladder and tummy empty. Later, when your puppy's body matures, and it has greater ability to hold in its urine, you are free to leave water with it all day. For now, controlling your puppy's water intake will speed up the housebreaking process. So always remember to water the pup first, *then* walk it.

Establishing Parameters

Yes, housebreaking requires a rigorous schedule, but it's the most effective way to establish for your puppy, right from the beginning, that the only acceptable bathroom is outdoors. When the pup is sixteen weeks old, it can graduate to a less stringent schedule. You'll be able to eliminate the 9:00 A.M. and 3:00 P.M. walks, and do only a 6:00 A.M., noon, 6:00 P.M., and 10:30 P.M. schedule. By this time, you've already established a pattern that will be the dog's way of life for the next six months. Work out the schedule that works best for both you and your dog. It's up to you to make sure that's *never less than four walks per day.* The positive reinforcement of this training method conditions the dog to work with its owner and to relieve itself within a reasonable time frame. Once we begin training, I'll tell you how to make your dog relieve itself on schedule and on command. But it's up to you, the owner, to be responsible for establishing a humane schedule. While I don't like to overanthropomorphize dogs, I always try to consider how I would feel in the dog's place. It gives a better perspective on what is, and what isn't, humane.

If you work and simply can't devote that kind of time to housebreaking, I urge you to find a competent and compassionate caretaker on whom you can depend completely. If you have no family member who can take on the job, ask your vet to recommend someone reliable. Remember, once you've taught your dog that outdoors is the only acceptable place for him to relieve himself, it's absolutely up to you, his responsible Alpha leader, to be there to take him out. Of course, if you have a fenced outdoor enclosure with a doggie door, you're home free!

Chapter 6

A Pup from the Pound

Many people aren't the least bit concerned about their dog's pedigree. They just want a good old all-American dog. The best place to find that is the local animal shelter, where wonderful dogs—including many with pedigrees—are waiting for homes. Adopting a shelter dog brings an automatic reward: the wonderful, heartwarming feeling that comes with saving a valuable life. *Fifteen million dogs are abandoned each and every year,* most of them to certain death and usually through no fault of their own. That's often the sad result when someone purchases a dog on impulse, without considering the commitment involved. Such people believe, wrongly, that owning a dog is all about love and nothing to do with discipline. They forgo the training and setting of parameters that are integral to a loving, responsible relationship. Since a dog that isn't taught is a dog that doesn't learn, problems inevitably result and when they do, these irresponsible owners simply throw up their hands and either turn the animal over to a shelter (and the euthanasia that usually follows), or abandon the dog altogether—almost a worse fate. Either way, it's the innocent dog that winds up the loser. That's one reason a great many caring people have vowed never to purchase a dog again—they'd rather give a needy shelter animal a home. Trouble is, if you adopt the dog, *you* inherit the problems someone else created, and those problems that are the result of careless "parenting" may take time, training, and enormous patience to correct.

Adopting a shelter dog is a bit like entering into a mail-order marriage. You're committing to sharing your life with someone you just met and know absolutely nothing about, and you're in the relationship for the long haul. It's a pretty daunting thought, especially since most of these dogs have no available history, leaving you with no clue as to past behavior. Add to that the fact that the shelter experience itself may have been so traumatic that the dog you see isn't necessarily the dog you'll get. There are, however, tricks that will let you hedge your bets. Just as choosing a pup from a breeder is easier when you know what questions to ask and what "tests" to perform, so it is at the shelter. We'll use some of those same tried-and-true techniques to help you determine (before you sign the "marriage" certificate) whether the shelter dog you've fallen in love with will be problematic or perfect. The best protection against a wrong choice is knowledge and a clear understanding of the positives and negatives.

Many of my clients who've adopted pets (including those who had always owned purebreds) swear that a dog rescued from death row is the most devoted, affectionate, seemingly grateful pet on the planet. Most say they'd never buy a dog again. It's such a gratifying experience to take an animal from the terrors of a shelter into a new and loving home. It's also an inexpensive way to acquire a great dog. Most shelters charge minimal fees—between $20 and $75 to cover the cost of shots and vaccinations—and with luck you might even find a purebred. I've seen Poodles, Labradors, German Shepherds, and Bichon Frises adopted from shelters, and many of them developed into elegant examples of their breeds. Of course, the majority of shelter dogs are all-American mutts, mixed breeds with a bit of this and a little of that in their DNA. That can be a positive. Cross-breeding often creates a stronger gene pool, resulting in fewer genetic problems. It also can create adorable, one-of-a-kind dogs (just take a look at Benji!) which is why the mutt remains a popular favorite in films, television, and commercials. Since mixed breeds tend to be savvy and street smart, they're often easier to train.

I trust that before making the decision to take a shelter dog into your life, you've already considered your lifestyle and decided whether you need an apartment-size dog with a tranquil personality or a big, rangy retriever who'll be your rough-and-tough companion on long walks through the woods. Matching lifestyles is the best formula for a loving, wonderful relationship that lasts a lifetime. With adoption you have an additional alternative: an older dog. While those cute puppies licking your hand are always the most appealing, they might not be the best choice for you. If, for example, you're a single person with a stressful job and little time, housebreaking can be a difficult process. An older dog probably will be housebroken already (as a rule, dogs learn not to soil their own homes), but even if not, the process generally will be quicker and easier than with a pup. And there'll be none of the chewing problems and destructive behavior that are part of puppyhood, since the older dog will have settled into a more adult, calm lifestyle. A mature dog is a terrific choice, and a wonderful companion as well, for older people who have neither the patience nor stamina to train a puppy. Before you make that first visit to the shelter, consider the options, then decide the *kind* of relationship you want with your dog. That's the first step towards getting it.

The Visit

If you're a tender-hearted person, the shelter experience can be distressing—row upon row of sad-eyed dogs, locked into cages, waiting for some loving person to rescue them. It's difficult not to want to take every single one home with you. Stop right there! You're there to adopt *one* dog, the right dog for you, and no matter how heartbreaking it might be to leave the others, it's the right thing to do. To take the emotional edge off the experience, and give you the support you need to make a clear-headed, intelligent choice, I suggest you take along a friend or family member. Besides, a second opinion is always useful.

If a shelter is upsetting to you, imagine how the dog feels. He's confused, lost, frightened. His family has left him and he doesn't understand why. In fact, he doesn't even really understand where he is. Once he had a loving home, familiar surroundings, and freedom; now he's locked in a cage. Worse yet, he may be in a holding cell with a group of other dogs, some of them bullies. If he's going to survive, he'll have to learn to protect himself. He may have to fight for his food. He develops fear, hostility, and anger, all qualities that show up later as aggression and may affect his finding a new home. He's also been deprived of loving human contact. Sadly, shelter personnel only have time to meet his basic needs of food, water, and medicine, and if a volunteer does come to offer a few minutes of play, she always goes away again, leaving him there alone again in his cage, feeling even more dejected and confused.

He may have developed medical problems from poor care, living on the street, or even from being in the shelter for too long, since diseases are a given in an overcrowded environment. He's a sad case, and for all you know, he's just an unresponsive, sad dog—not the kind you'd enjoy having around. You could be right, or you could be passing up a perfectly wonderful dog. This is where asking the right questions and performing the right DogSpeak tests will help you either make a perfect match or a perfectly terrible mistake. The perfect match is what we aim for!

Making the Right Choice

When you visit the shelter, ask to take an inspection tour of the cages to see all the dogs available. This lets you narrow your choices to a manageable four or five possibilities. Unfortunately, some facilities, especially those that are overcrowded and understaffed, don't allow visitors into the shelter area but will bring the dogs out to you. In that case, ask to see the type of dog you're looking for. Whether you see all the dogs together, or only a pre-picked selection, *never* be tempted to take a dog that isn't what you predetermined you need. For instance, if you want a tiny lap dog and the only dogs available are shepherd size, walk away and come back another day. The shelter population is always changing and it's better to leave home empty-handed than to take home the wrong pet. If you have to return it, you'll double the trauma to the dog and add some stress to your adoption experience as well.

If you are allowed into the shelter area, walk each row slowly and methodically, making eye contact with any dog that appeals to you. Chances are, if your dog is there, you'll spot it—that certain connection, the look that says, "Please take me home!" That doesn't mean it *is* the right dog for you, but it's a start. When you think you've found "your dog," ask to take him to a private spot where you can look him over carefully and meet him on more intimate terms. Look into his eyes. Are they bright, intelligent, alert? Does he come to greet you or back away in fear? Ask questions. Is the dog on medication? Has he been eating well? Has he been sick? If he seems quiet and withdrawn, this may well be the cause. If you're torn between several choices, bring each dog out individually and test its reactions using these simple tests, all the while making sure your gestures are never threatening.

- Create a loud noise by clapping your hands or dropping a book. (Drop it, don't throw it!) If the dog has no response, it may be deaf.
- Gesture for the dog to come to you. If it doesn't, it may not see well.
- Make shadows on the wall and sudden movements. Then watch to see whether the dog is skittish, which could indicate a panic syndrome.
- If the shelter permits, walk the dog outside for a half-block or so, to see how it performs on-leash. One of my clients adopted an adorable dog only to find the animal agoraphobic, so terrified of being outside that it shivered and shook each time she walked it. Since the shelter didn't permit her to walk it outdoors, she never knew until she'd already become an adoptive parent. It took years of training to manage the problem.
- Bring a squeaky toy along and toss it to the dog. Do his ears prick up, his eyes light up? He's letting you know, in DogSpeak, that he's alert and intelligent. Does he happily jump on the toy and play with it, or bring it to you? He's saying in DogSpeak that he understands the fun of a game, and he's ready and willing to interact with you. If he runs away, he may be overly fearful, with serious problems that later will become yours. They may be solvable, but be pre-

pared to put in the time and effort unless you want a dog that bolts at any unexpected sound. Of course, with a shelter dog, it's always difficult to know whether a fear response is genetic or simply the result of shelter trauma.

- If you've chosen a smaller dog, try cradling it in your arms. If the dog struggles or resists, it's a DogSpeak warning that he's either frightened or somewhat dominant, a trait which can develop into aggressive behavior. Since you don't really know what's happened to the dog in his former life, this is a hard one to assess. But if the dog lies comfortably and quietly in your arms, it's a clear indication he views you as Alpha and will accept you as leader of his pack. That's where every good owner/dog relationship begins.

- Touch and massage the dog. Touch is a universally understood language among wolves and dogs, confirming bona fide members of the pack. Pick up the dog's paws and touch its toes. This is the kind of thing children do and therefore a good test for a family with kids. If the dog accepts your touch, and appears to like it, you're speaking the same language. If he stiffens and snaps, that's a bad sign, though it may not necessarily indicate aggression. He may be in pain. (There's *always* a reason for snapping.) Nevertheless, this response indicates problems you shouldn't have to assume, and no matter how difficult it may be to leave that adorable but aggressive dog behind, you owe it to yourself and your family to be realistic and sensible. You can't adopt every dog that needs a home; just the one that's right for you.

If the dog you like has passed all the tests, you're free to fall in love. It would be just too sad to give your heart to the cutest little pup in the place, only to discover serious emotional problems that would make it the worst possible choice. We've just eliminated that possibility and you and your dog can begin to form one of the most important love relationships of your life, that spiritual link between dog and man that's as old as time.

Needless to say, you won't just walk out with your dog; there'll be all the necessary paperwork. Some shelters require personal recommendations, from friends who can attest to your ability to care for a dog. You'll be asked to sign a form that guarantees you will neuter the dog within a given period of time, usually one month. This assures the shelter that your dog's progeny won't turn up at their facility somewhere down the road. (Most shelters will provide you with a voucher and a list of veterinary clinics that will honor it with a reduced rate for neutering.) You'll also find that most veterinarians offer reduced fees, even free first visits, for adopted pets. You will pay a minimal fee for the vaccinations and shots the shelter has given. However, I always recommend that you take the dog *immediately* to a veterinarian for a private checkup. Your vet may decide to revaccinate (some don't quite trust the freshness of the shelter's vaccine) and give the dog additional protective shots. Some shelters give you nylon leash-and-collar combos to set you on your way. But be careful: These were not designed to restrain a large, strong dog. Get your dog his own gear the moment you get him home!

Home with Your Newly Adopted Friend

I hope you've planned ahead, because pound pups need a room of their own just like the most pampered pedigreed pooch. The shelter dog has been through an unnerving experience and, even more than any other dog, needs a safe, secure place of its own. Of course, preparing your adopted dog's room is a bit more difficult. That's because, when you head for the shelter, you have no idea what kind of dog you'll bring home or even whether you'll find a suitable dog on the first visit. (And remember: If you don't find the dog that fits your lifestyle, *don't* be tempted to take an inappropriate one that you may have to return to the shelter. That would be too hard on you both.) Even if you do find the perfect dog, you couldn't have known its size in advance, which means that many of the tools in your Dog Owner's Starter Kit will have to wait until you actually own your dog. However, you *can* decide where you'll locate the dog's room, the space where he'll have his crate, his food and water bowls, and his toys. That's a start. Eventually you'll need everything in the Starter Kit, including crate, leash, control collar, and food and water bowls. More than likely, you and your new canine companion will leave the shelter with only the nylon collar/leash they gave you, so you should head at once for the nearest pet-supply store to buy a properly fitting collar, a control collar, leash, and that indispensable tool, a crate.

In the space you've chosen as the dog's room, place its crate, water and food bowls, and toys. If you've adopted a puppy, please follow all the micro-training guidelines in the previous chapter. Your new canine friend comes to you with no training history. In fact, you won't even know if he's housebroken. It's up to you to begin a new life pattern, complete with training schedule, feeding schedule, walk schedule, and playtime. We'll begin at the beginning, using my proven techniques for making the dog feel secure and establishing a reliable schedule on which it can depend. Now, more than ever, you have the opportunity to establish a uniquely close bond between you and your adopted canine companion.

You may be lucky and find a young puppy that hasn't been traumatized by the shelter experience, letting you start the relationship with a clean slate. But odds are you'll come home with an older dog looking for a second chance with a new and more compassionate owner. That's just what you'll need to be: understanding and compassionate. Please don't ever forget that a shelter dog has been through a lot, and use plenty of patience and loads of love to reassure him that this time is forever. This is a perfect opportunity for both of you to begin a new, supremely happy life!

As you head for home with your dog, try to put yourself in his place. He's been through the mill. He's lost his former owner, and probably feels lost himself. For all you know, he may have been abused by a succession of owners, or been adopted and then, all too sadly, returned to the lonely shelter life. One thing is almost certain: This dog is bound to be frightened and confused. He needs time to regain his composure and, above all else, he needs *gentle* love and affection from a master and family who will make him feel secure. You can start the process even before you get home by walking your new dog around your neighborhood to accustom him to his new territory (unless, of course, you've adopted a very young pup that still doesn't have its final shots). Let him sniff the unfamiliar scents, read the DogSpeak signs left by other dogs, and urine-mark what will be, from this day on, his new home. Your dog will have given a DogSpeak message to all the neighborhood dogs that there's a new kid on the block, and he'll feel far more secure on the next walk, when he recognizes his own scent.

Beware of a too-emotional family welcome. As you might imagine, your dog probably feels overwhelmed already. Introduce him to his new family quietly and gently. There'll be plenty of time for excitement later on, after he's had a chance to settle in and feel at home.

You may discover, later on, that the dog you brought home isn't the one you finally get. Some dogs are so shelter-shocked that they don't begin to blossom for weeks, even months. One of my clients adopted a shelter dog who, for the first month, never barked. She began to worry that perhaps it had no voice. I reassured her that the dog probably was afraid to bark. As it began to grow secure in its new home, it became a wonderful watchdog, alert to every unusual noise or approaching stranger and voicing the alarm, loud and clear. So please be prepared to soothe the jangled nerves of a dog that's had a hard life. Being dumped in a shelter is *no fun.*

First Things First

As soon as you get home, feed and water your dog. Shelter meals are spartan and a dog is lucky to get one square meal a day. In fact, you'll probably find that your dog will gain weight rapidly once it's on a good, healthy diet. Many shelter-dog owners say their pets doubled their weight within six months, a point to consider when you're picking out your dog.

If it's possible to see your veterinarian on that very first day, please do so, but *don't wait longer than two days.* You need to pick up any potential problems that may be brewing and nip them in the bud. Your veterinarian will give you a complete rundown on the state of your dog's health and may give a booster rabies shot and other inoculations as well. He also will suggest an appropriate diet, to get your dog started on the road to blooming good health. Ask the doctor for a feeding schedule and have him recommend the appropriate food for your dog, which will vary according to the dog's age and health.

Since you don't know whether the shelter dog is housebroken, it's best to assume that he isn't. Though you may be tempted to give the dog the run of the house immediately, that's the *wrong* thing to do. Establishing behavior parameters right at the outset will prevent behavior problems down the road. For a young puppy, you need the complete course of micro-training described in the previous chapter, using the crate to confine the pup in a small space until it's completely housebroken. With an adult dog, you have a bit more freedom but you still should confine it in the crate for a few days until you're sure. The crate also will serve as insurance against destructive behaviors, such as chewing or separation anxiety, which may be triggered by the anxiety of coming into a brand-new home with total strangers. As you might imagine, a shelter dog probably will have mixed feelings about anything that resembles a cage—after all, he's been confined in one, alone with no human affection and minimal contact, for weeks, even as long as a year, and walked (if he's lucky) once a day during cage-cleaning. (Shelters are not inhumane, just overworked and understaffed.) Naturally, the dog isn't thrilled by the prospect of another "cage." It's up to you, his new owner and loving Alpha, to make this next crate experience a positive one by establishing a reliable schedule. Soon your dog will view the crate as its safety net and den.

Begin by confining the dog in the crate with a few chew toys, removing it *at least four times per day* for feeding, watering, walking, play, and just plain love. The perfect walk schedule—morning, noon, 6:00 P.M. and 10:00 to 11:00 P.M.—should continue from three to five days. After that time, begin expanding the dog's space, keeping him confined in a kitchen or other mid-size room while still maintaining the established walk schedule. Soon you will have developed a regular routine that cues your dog to the correct times to relieve himself. If your dog regresses and soils the floor, confine him again, using the same walk schedule, until he's gotten the message.

Please don't forget to allow time for play and love. A shelter dog really needs affection. Join in his games, tell him you love him and that you think he's wonderful. You'll be surprised to see your dog bloom right before your eyes. Soon your bewildered shelter dog will learn that you are someone on whom he can depend and the transformation you'll see, as the days go by, will make all the effort worthwhile. Once your dog has learned the rules of good behavior—no messing in the house and no destructive habits—you're free to have fun . . . together.

To the Rescue

Shelters aren't the only source for homeless dogs. Breed-specific rescue organizations or "leagues" are a wonderful way to acquire a pedigreed dog that, for whatever reason, has found itself homeless. Perhaps its long-time owner has died, or become ill and unable to continue caring for it. As you've already seen, responsible breeders always are concerned about making sure this doesn't happen to their dogs, but occasionally one slips through the safety net. That's when a breed's rescue organization goes into gear. Working as a close-knit community, rescue organizations serve as an effective network in saving pedigreed dogs who have lost, or are in danger of losing, their homes. The Greyhound Rescue Organization has done a commendable job in finding homes for older racing dogs who, when this organization stepped in, were being put down by the score, once age diminished their racing speeds.

Rescue organizations also work closely with the staff at shelters, who often telephone these groups when purebreds turn up at their facility. As a rule, rescue organizations place rescued dogs in foster homes until permanent homes can be found. Dogs placed by these organizations usually have been checked by a veterinarian. The only cost the new owner will incur is the reimbursement of any medical fees or expenses to the organization.

The best way to locate any breed's rescue organization is through that breed's club. Again, you'll find the addresses of each breed's club available at the American Kennel Club's New York headquarters. I can think of no more gratifying way to acquire a purebred dog. You'll not only get the breed of your choice—which means you'll have some inkling of its genetic programming—but you'll be saving a life as well. Knowing and understanding the characteristics of the breed will make the period of adjustment somewhat easier for you both. But one pathetic fact remains: The dog has been given up. It's feeling lost, lonely, and confused and needs every bit as much love and attention as the shelter dog. Your understanding of its heritage will give you a valuable head start on making it feel secure again, and help you return it to its birthright as a dog of great lineage.

Chapter 7

The Vocabulary of DogSpeak

It's impossible for us humans, with our limited sensory abilities, even to comprehend the hyperacute senses of our dog companions. From their supersensitive noses to their ultrasonic hearing, our dogs have left us far behind in the sensory communications race. We even find it difficult to believe that our dogs can read the entire history of a dog passerby just by sniffing the drops of urine he's left on a lamppost. Body language, on the other hand, is quite another matter. It's a language we humans have used and understood since babyhood. After all, it's through body language and gestures that we communicate with people who don't speak our own language.

As with learning any language, we first must learn the alphabet, the vocabulary, the rules of grammar, the syntax, and the idioms required before we can carry on a meaningful conversation in DogSpeak. That begins with understanding our dog's body language, from his facial expression to his stance. If you've ever played charades, you'll know exactly how much information can be transmitted through body language alone. Gestures and facial expressions have an amazing ability to communicate moods, needs, desires, and emotions. In fact, an entire psychological subculture has developed around body language and its hidden meanings. There's no question that body language is the primer of DogSpeak, our most readily available means of communicating with our pets in language *they* will understand. You'll find that each expression, each body posture, each gesture of a paw collaborates to deliver a clearly "worded" DogSpeak message. And just as with humans, the most easily read part of a dog's body language is his face. Facial expressions convey extraordinarily accurate meanings and are as varied in your dog as they are in your best friend.

Facial Expressions

A dog's face, just like a person's, is the most expressive part of his body. But unlike humans, who basically rely on the eyes and mouth to deliver an expressive message, dogs use every part of their heads to convey both emotion and motivation. Once you're fluent in DogSpeak, you'll be able to know, by the look in your dog's eyes, the position of his ears, the wrinkle of his muzzle, whether he's poised to lick a stranger's hand or seriously bite it. If you have a dog prone to aggression, that's exceedingly valuable information.

Dogs' eyes show an astonishing range of expressions, from fear to aggression to laughter (yes!) to sadness to love. (Look into your own dog's eyes right now for a firsthand example.) The position of a dog's ears has unmistakable meaning to other dogs, issuing a clear DogSpeak message that says, "I'm the king here," "I'm worried you might not be friendly," or, "Hi, Buddy, great day!" Each flick of the ear is a clear indicator of mood, intent, and hierarchical rank. A dog's mouth, just like a human's, can express humor, sadness, aggression, or alertness. The nose sniffs to acquire information. The muzzle wrinkles in a sneer, draws back in a snarl, moves forward in an alert or relaxes into a canine smile. In all cases, the tiniest adjustment of these expressions may indicate a change in the dog's mood or intentions. And with DogSpeak, reading the nuances may mean the difference between a friendly encounter or a nasty confrontation.

Since the best way to recognize each expression and its accompanying message is to see it, I'll demonstrate here the full range of a dog's facial expressions, which are identical with those of his wolf ancestors. I'll also show you those variations of expression that result from selective breeding, with which we humans have created dogs that differ greatly from their wolf forebears—dogs with flat muzzles, drooping ears, or even no tails. And we've further complicated the issue by our own "cosmetic surgery"—docked tails, clipped ears. As a result, we've created "dialects" which also must be learned, if becoming fluent in DogSpeak is the goal.

The Ears Say . . .

Ears pricked and pointed straight up indicate a variety of moods and emotions, ranging from alertness, dominance, playfulness, curiosity, eagerness, and excitement to aggression. Pricked ears also may indicate that one of the central factors of pack behavior—the chase and hunt mode—is about to kick in. This is useful information if you're walking your dog on a loose leash and he's spied a squirrel in the distance that you haven't seen. But if pricked-up ears can convey so many different messages, how can you tell the differences? *By putting the ears in context with all other parts of a dog's "speech,"* from the eyes to the muzzle to the body posture to the vocalization. That's true DogSpeak, the language you'll learn after you've got the

The face of an alert dog: ears pricked up ("Hi, who are you?"), eyes wide and sparkling ("Good to see you!"), mouth relaxed, open, and possibly panting ("What shall we do today?").

basic vocabulary down pat. For now, concentrate on your dog's ears.

When he hears an unaccustomed sound, or spots something interesting such as an approaching animal or bouncing ball, your dog's ears will stand at attention, pricked and alert. If the sound is interesting enough, he may revolve his ears outward, to receive even more information, still keeping them pricked. And if he cocks his head from side to side, he's saying in DogSpeak, "Could you run that by me again?" But let's say you own a Cocker Spaniel with drooping ears. Watch him closely when you make an unusual sound and you'll see that the part of his ear closest to the head is raised to the alert position while the leather of the ear—the droopy part—extends slightly outward, elephant style. That's Cocker Spaniel DogSpeak dialect for "Alert!"

A different face of alert: ears pricked but revolved to receive new information ("What's that strange noise?"), eyes wide and alert ("I'd better look for it"), mouth closed to allow sniffing ("Gotta smell this one out!"), and nose actively sniffing ("I think I've caught the scent").

The face of a relaxed dog: ears halfway back and slightly outward ("Great day for lazing around"), eyes open and calm ("Wonder what's on the agenda?"), and mouth open and relaxed ("Maybe after my nap we can go for a run").

A relaxed dog will hold his ears at half-mast—lowered and pointing slightly backward, like the wings of a Boeing 707. As a rule, it's pretty easy to see when your dog is completely relaxed, and when he is, that's a good time to memorize the ear position. In the case of droopy-eared dogs, the ears hang loosely at the side like a pair of furry earrings.

Dominant aggression—ears pricked, eyes narrowed, muzzle snarling and showing teeth ("I warn you, one more move and I'll bite").

Aggression places the ears in two distinct positions: The first pricks the ears up and forward to the alert position; the second, the attack mode, rotates the ears to the side and close to the head for protection, giving the opponent less opportunity to grab onto them. It's crucially important to read both positions, since if an attack is on the way, you certainly want to get out of its path. (If it's your own dog on the attack, this is your DogSpeak message to get him under control, and *quickly!*)

Anxiety, which often precedes fear: ears laid partially back ("I'm not sure you're friendly"), eyes slightly narrowed ("I'm getting nervous"), and mouth closed and tense ("I'm ready to react").

Fear, including apprehension or anxiety, has its DogSpeak expression in ears laid back and flattened against the skull, identical to the ear placement in aggression. Indeed, fear often is followed by aggression, which even has its own name, fear-aggression. The difference lies in the other areas of a fearful dog's expression, making it especially important to read its eyes and the position of its muzzle as well if you want to avoid being bitten. I'll show you next how to read those expressions.

The Eyes Say . . .

Dogs can be as wide-eyed with excitement as humans. Eyes opened wide are the DogSpeak indicators for alertness, focus, friendliness, or happiness and are always noted just before a chase. But wide-open eyes also may indicate a challenge. So how do you interpret the correct DogSpeak message? By checking out two simple factors—blinking or staring—which let you interpret the DogSpeak message accurately. For example, a dog eager for his owner to play may have alert, wide-open eyes accompanied by a bit of flirtatious blinking, while a dog intent on showing he's boss will have his eyes wide, alert, and fully open, accompanied by a stare that says, "You'd better back off, because I won't!" Staring, in fact, *always* indicates dominance, and dominance, all too often, is followed by aggression. Your dog is thinking, "If I'm gonna stay top dog, I can't let this guy challenge my authority." As Alpha, neither can you, which is why reading the stare is one of your most important tools in staying on top of a potentially explosive dominance situation.

Narrowed eyes indicate anxiety, fear, or submission.

Eyes that are narrowed slightly may mirror anxiety, submission, fear, or suspicion. At times, they even may convey a threat. What's important in determining the precise meaning is the accompanying ear position. A dog showing its submission to a more dominant dog may narrow its eyes and avert its gaze, while placing its ears in the submissive laid-back posture. That's a crystal-clear DogSpeak message that says, "I'm yours to do with as you see fit." Aggression's narrowed eyes, on the other hand, are accompanied by a challenging stare and ears flattened against the skull. This says, all too clearly in DogSpeak, "I'm gonna kill you!" As you can see, it's supremely important to understand the differences so that you will know, beyond doubt, whether your dog is saying "Whatever you want, Boss," or "Don't come one step closer!" Only then can you adjust your responses to the situation at hand and maintain the control that is your Alpha mandate.

The Muzzle and Mouth Say . . .

A dog, just like a person, expresses itself eloquently with its mouth and lips. But a dog uses another body part that most humans can't: its muzzle. If a dog wrinkles its muzzle into a snarl, draws its lips back to bare its canine teeth and gives every indication that those teeth are ready to snap, it's a message of aggression that's hard to miss. Other DogSpeak messages are more subtle. Fear often imitates aggression, and a fearful dog may draw his lips back to expose teeth. But what differentiates this from true aggression is the accompanying position of the ears, which remain laid back in the fear mode.

A dog announcing that he's top dog, or Alpha, begins his announcement with a slightly open mouth, which slowly progresses to curled. (It's the canine equivalent of a superior smirk.) If dominance is taken to the extreme, the muzzle draws back in the unmistakable expression of aggression. A submissive dog, on the other hand, pulls its mouth back into a canine

Dominant aggression—ears pricked, eyes narrowed, muzzle snarling and showing teeth ("I warn you, one more move and I'll bite").

The face of fear aggression—ears laid back, eyes narrow, muzzle snarling ("I'm scared but I'll try to protect myself").

The face of submission—ears back, eyes averted, mouth pulled back ("You're the leader and I'll do whatever you say").

Guarding aggression—ears turned outward ("I heard a danger"), eyes narrowed ("I mean business"), muzzle pulled back to show teeth ("Get off my property!").

"grin" while nuzzling or licking its dominant partner, animal *or* person, in the face—a clear DogSpeak message that says, "You're better than I am and I know it." You can be sure that a dog with a submissive expression is ready to take orders, whether from you, his Alpha, or any other dog on the block.

A dog guarding its territory, its bone, or its food will open its mouth slightly, baring the teeth and occasionally snapping. It's DogSpeak for "Watch out!" and is a menacing message you must take seriously. An anxious dog, on the other hand, will keep its lips closed and pulled back into a "grin," sometimes accompanied by panting or drooling. That's a dead giveaway that he's nervous as all get-out and hopes you, or the dog with you, won't give him any trouble.

An eager, excited dog may have its mouth open, but keep its teeth covered, saying in DogSpeak, "I'm just out here having a blast; you have nothing to fear from me." On the other hand, a friendly, playful dog usually has a relaxed, slightly open mouth drawn back into a canine smile. That's a DogSpeak message that's hard to miss. Check out your own dog the next time you say to him, "Get ready, Buster, we're going for a run!" and you'll see what I mean.

If you've got a flat-muzzle dog, such as a Bulldog, Boxer, Pug, or Pekingese, then you're going to have to adjust your muzzle interpretations somewhat. These breeds have an extended jaw that alters their expressions. However, flat-muzzle breeds compensate for that by pulling their lips up rather than back to bare their often formidable teeth. After all, they don't have a lot of lip to work with! What they do have is the ability to make a lot of snorting, threatening noises that get their message across quite effectively and to use their massive jaws and prominent teeth to look super-menacing. As for grinning, any owner will know that these dogs appear to grin most of the time, so if you really want to catch the DogSpeak message, watch their other

Aggression as seen in a flat-muzzle dog.

signals to find out what they're saying and what action they may intend to take. Knowing your dog's moves as soon as he does is a huge plus in maintaining your Alpha status!

Body Language

Just check out your fellow humans to note the difference stance makes. A confident person walks with a buoyant step, head held high, arms swinging freely. A timid person, on the other hand, may keep his head down, with arms held into his sides as he walks with hesitant steps. From a swagger to a slink, our stance impacts those who observe us, telling them in no uncertain terms that we're sure of ourselves, blustery, meek, fearful, or confused. Muggers know this all too well, and use it effectively to choose the timid and inattentive as easy prey. Absolutely nothing telegraphs more information about us than our body postures. The same applies to dogs, and it's in his body posture that you'll see the true personality of your dog.

The Stance States . . .

The DogSpeak stance has two polar-opposite extremes: the dominant "I'm in charge" stance and the submissive "I'll do anything you say" stance, with an entire range of postures in between. Both extremes, constant dominance and complete submission, are genetically programmed and potentially problematic, and it was to help you avoid those extreme personalities that I developed my test for choosing a perfect pup. Well-balanced dogs have the complete range of dominance-submission postures in their vocabulary. And just as we humans display different personalities to the different people around us, depending on the closeness of the relationship (the personality you show to your husband, wife, or children probably is quite different from that seen by your employer, your best friend, or a total stranger), so dogs take on different stances with different canine counterparts, depending on each individual relationship. First, that relationship must be established.

A dominant dog, like the Alpha wolf, announces his status immediately by his unmistakably superior stance: head high, ears erect and rotated slightly outward, body pulled to full height, tail high and waving, and a rather stiff walk that says clearly in DogSpeak, "I'm the top dog around here." He not only says, he means it. This isn't bluster, it's dominance, and it's something to be taken seriously.

A submissive dog, on the other hand, approaches a strange dog in a more hesitant manner: He holds his body lower, and his tail hangs lower as well. It's perfectly clear to any observer, including the submissive dog, just who's boss in the relationship. Generally, when two strange dogs approach one another, there's a neutral moment to determine just which is the dominant dog. As they approach, both will take a noncombative stance: ears forward, muzzles nose-to-nose, tails at half-mast.

The stance of a dominant dog—tall, proud, ears pricked, head and tail high, fur fluffed up.

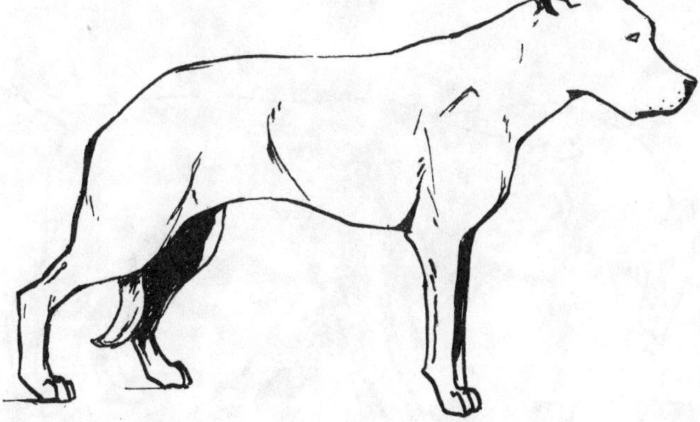

The stance of a submissive dog—ears laid back, tail tucked between legs.

The stance of a relaxed, confident dog—tail straight out, head up.

Then the get-acquainted dance begins, the ritual that will establish each dog's position and role in the relationship. Like two boxers sizing each other up in the ring, the dogs circle each other, first sniffing each other's muzzles, then genitals, reading

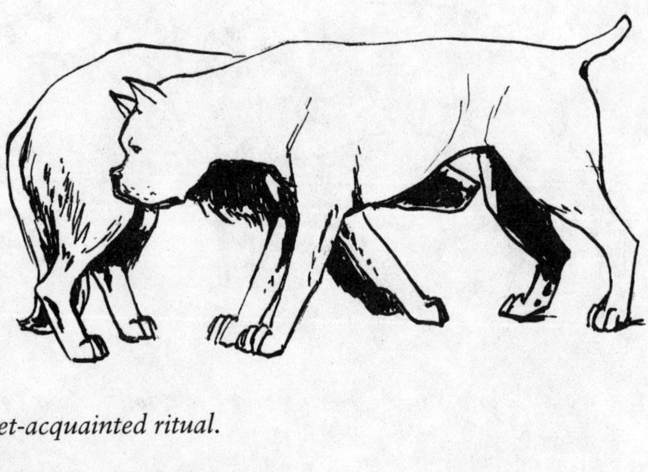

The get-acquainted ritual.

one another's scent (which in the dominant dog is invariably stronger) and body language. It's a law of DogSpeak that this ritual involves a truce during which neither dog attacks. Once the sizing-up is completed, the relationship gets under way. In some instances, one dog may tuck its tail between its legs, denying the other its genitals. Since this clearly signifies submission,

A submissive dog bows to an Alpha ("I acknowledge you're the leader and I submit to you").

the DogSpeak message is, "I won't even challenge you; I know you're king." But if the two dogs are more or less of equal rank in the canine hierarchy, the less dominant dog will be eager to please but unwilling to submit. This dog will flatten its ears, narrow or squint its eyes, and either nudge the more dominant dog's muzzle or lick its lips, as if to say, "I think you're terrific!" It's a DogSpeak version of hero-worship in action. In some cases, the more dominant dog may view the submissive dog with complete contempt, remaining aloof now that his dominance is clear and the situation is under *his* control. (You know how that goes: "What a wimp! Who needs him for a pal!") On the other hand, he may allow a friendship to develop by giving a DogSpeak message that says, "Perhaps we can be friends." He does this by closing his eyes slightly, drawing his ears back a bit, and turning his head to expose his throat. The DogSpeak message is, "I trust you, and so I'll let you hang out with my crowd."

When both dogs are dominant, the more dominant dog may lay claim to his Alpha position with a furious fight, grabbing the other dog's ear and forcing the dog onto its back, belly up. In a situation like this, one dog is likely to be hurt. Reading the nuances and signals of dominant-submissive behavior will give you a DogSpeak idiom which lets you, the Alpha/owner, avoid nasty and dangerous fights. This is one of the most important grammar lessons you'll ever learn! If you read the DogSpeak signs correctly, and spot a dominant dog approaching your dominant dog, the wisest move is to keep your dog in check on a short leash, and leave the scene to avoid confrontation.

A submissive dog greets a dominant dog ("I won't tread on your turf").

Two confident dogs meet ("Hi! Who are you?").

The Tail Telegraphs . . .

There's no more eloquent aspect of DogSpeak than the language of the tail, that high-wagging banner that telegraphs to the world just exactly what your dog is seeing, feeling, sensing, and saying. The tail has an enormous range of expressions, each with its own clearly stated message.

A dog uses his tail to reinforce messages that simultaneously are being transmitted by his facial expressions and body language. The tail delivers its DogSpeak messages in three ways: position, shape, and movement. A high, erect, and bristling (the better to make it look bigger) tail generally shows self-confidence or dominance, while a tail carried low indicates submission. When two strange dogs meet, their tails are held straight out, in a neutral position, until one dog establishes his dominance and raises his tail/banner to the high-flying "I'm Alpha" position. A relaxed tail means "all is well," but a tail hanging low indicates concern, confusion, worry, or depression. When a dog's tail is tucked close to the hindquarters, and his legs are lowered in a slightly crouched position, the Dog-

Speak message is "You don't have to worry, I know you're the boss." A tail tucked entirely between the legs shows the complete submission of a dog at the bottom of the canine order, a completely defeated dog. That's the Omega of the wolf pack, and it isn't a position any dog would want!

Tail movements also telegraph feelings and attitudes: a loose, freely wagging tail usually shows friendliness. Submissive dogs may wag their entire hindquarters with a slightly pulled-in tail. When a high-ranking dog approaches another of status, his tail will be carried high and vertical, with a slight trembling motion that says, beyond any doubt, "Don't mess with me, fella, I'm tops around here."

Highly submissive dogs and puppies may wag their tails tentatively while keeping them tucked between their legs, DogSpeak for complete and total submission. Apparently such wagging releases more of a puppy's or a submissive dog's scent, a tactic which appeals to parental instincts and pacifies any potentially threatening dominant dog.

A dog also uses its tail position to invite sniffing of its anal gland scent, either to establish a relationship or as a sexual invitation. A tail tucked between the legs denies another dog intimate knowledge.

As you become fluent in DogSpeak, you'll learn to read even the most subtle positions, shapes, and motions of your dog's tail, all of which, coupled with his other body language, tell you exactly what message he's trying to give you . . . and what he plans to do next. But what about those dogs whose tails are docked—dogs such as Cocker Spaniels, Bulldogs, or Poodles? Can they use their tails to communicate? As a rule, these dogs compensate by exaggerated body movements, often wagging the entire body instead of just the tail. It's more difficult to read a docked tail's signals, of course, but if you watch closely, you'll find that docked-tail dogs also use the universal tail language.

One of the greatest fallacies in dogdom is that a wagging

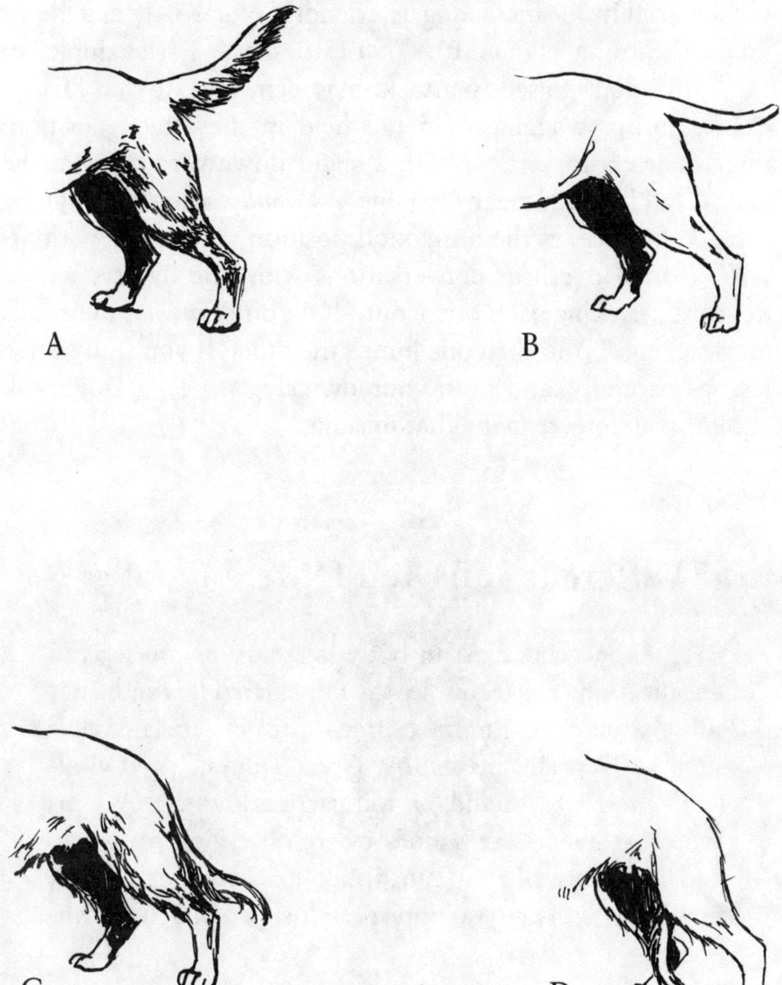

Tail positions can show whether a dog is . . .
(A) Confident
(B) Neutral, relaxed
(C) Cautious (or, in some breeds, relaxed)
(D) Fearful or submissive

tail invariably means a dog is friendly. *Not so!* It can be as much a warning as the rattles of a rattlesnake. For example, an aggressive dog, poised to attack, may demonstrate that fact by quick, abrupt wagging of a tail held in the attack position: three-quarters to vertical with a slight downward twist at the end. A tail like this means trouble, *especially* when it's wagging rapidly. It precedes the horizontal position that comes with attack. I often overhear conversations with dog owners whose dogs are checking each other out, "Oh, don't worry, their tails are wagging." And then one jumps the other. If you study these lessons carefully, and note your own dog's special DogSpeak accent, you'll never make that mistake.

Different Tails Tell Different Tales

Regional accents exist in body language as much as in vocalization. For example, the tail carried low indicates submission or fear in most breeds, but in certain breeds such as German Shepherds, Great Danes, Newfoundlands, and Greyhounds, a tail carried low simply indicates a relaxed state. Here's where observing your dog, and knowing all you can about his breed or mix of breeds, will help you interpret his personal tail language.

The Glands Give a Message . . .

Dogs use their glandular systems in amazing ways to communicate, a feat we humans can scarcely imagine. For example, have you ever seen your dog scratch the ground furiously after he relieves himself? And have you wondered why? He's releasing his personal, identifiable scent through scent glands between his toes, leaving the message "Buster was here" for every other dog on the block.

Their scent, and its distribution, is an essential means of communication for dogs. Each time your dog defecates, he releases a thick coating on his feces that's used to mark and establish his territory. This is why dogs sniff fresh feces, a habit we humans find offensive but which dogs use to discover who's come along and what their rank is. Have you ever seen your dog drag its rear end across the floor or lawn after relieving itself? Contrary to what many people believe, such an action doesn't necessarily indicate worms (though it may); the dog is forcing the anal glands to release their scent onto the ground for other dogs to note. And what other dogs will note is your dog's state of mind, his health, and his gender.

Puppies or submissive dogs being threatened by a dominant dog or held by a dominant person (being held down at the vet is a good example) may squirt their anal gland scent as a defense mechanism, just as a skunk does. Given the acrid, horrible smell, this tactic is one that works, generally stopping dogs and people in their tracks.

Other glands are located on the cheeks, just in front of the ears, as well as at the upper base of the tail. Undoubtedly you've seen dogs rub their rear ends against a tree or a wall, perhaps even the sofa, or rub their heads against your legs or a corner of the sofa. They aren't scratching their backs or their heads, but depositing their unmistakable and unique scent, marking the tree, the furniture, and you as their private property.

Besides the scent these glands release, dogs release additional scent in their urine. As you've already seen in "Primal DogSpeak," one drop of a dog's urine is potent enough to perfume 10,000 gallons of water! Every time your dog urinates on a lamppost, fire hydrant, or tree, he's marking his turf, letting every other neighborhood dog know that he's here, this is his property, keep off! With their exquisitely sensitive noses, dogs not only can read the signature scent of any dog that's marked with its urine but also can discern whether that dog was healthy and happy or stressed and aggressive when it left its urine message.

A dog's scent is his identity, which explains why when that scent is removed in a bath (something most dogs hate), he feels compelled to roll in something fragrant (that usually means "smelly" to us humans) in order to feel, and smell, like a dog again.

The Fur Announces . . .

Being "all puffed up" has a very real meaning in DogSpeak. Just check out your dog as he approaches a strange dog. If he's a self-confident, dominant dog, he'll pull himself up to full height (even if that means practically standing on tip-toe) and fluff his coat out visibly to be seen as bigger and "badder" to this strange dude. Watch your dog when he's barking furiously at what he supposes to be an intruder. You'll see his tail go straight up into a full and luxurious plume (providing, of course, his tail isn't docked), his chest visibly expand, and his hackles (the hairs on the back extending from the neck to the base of the tail) rise, telegraphing "I'm a serious threat, stay off my turf!" The idea is to make himself look as big and formidable as possible to any potential adversary, a bluff that usually pays off. (Like most bluffs, raised hackles also disguise a certain amount of insecurity.)

Dogs are remarkable in their use of their skin muscles, even their hair follicles, to transmit these clear DogSpeak messages to other dogs. We humans have the same inherent physical capabilities (consider how many times you've said "It makes my skin crawl" or "My hair stood on end"); unfortunately, we've forgotten how to use them.

The Phonetics of DogSpeak

When we tell a dog to "speak," we expect him to bark. But a bark is just a single element of vocalization, the complicated *spoken* language of dogs and one of the Eight Central Factors of Pack Behavior. Each sound a dog makes conveys a very specific DogSpeak message to another dog. It will to you as well, once you've got your DogSpeak vocabulary down pat. Just listen to your dog's sounds carefully. In a single day, depending on the canine company you meet, you might hear a soft, low growl, a sharp bark, a whine, a whimper, a yip, a howl, a snarl, and a series of sharp (and serious) barks that say quite clearly, "Stay where you are! Don't come any closer!" This is vocal DogSpeak and the better you understand it, the more completely you will understand your dog and what he may be planning.

Vocal DogSpeak consists of numerous variations on a bark, growl, howl, and whine or whimper, each with a wide range of meanings, depending on pitch, volume, and speed. For example, there is the deep, low-in-the-chest growl that immediately connotes aggression, or the low short growl that announces dominance. Five separate but recognizable barks convey aggression, anxiety, fear, warning, or even a wish to play. The variations of a whine range from the long rising-pitch whine of fear to the whimper of pups to the short, eagerly repeated whines that say, "Come on out and play." A howl can convey meanings ranging from loneliness to fear to the howl of a hound that announces, "I've treed the possum—come and see!"

Translating DogSpeak

The Bark Says . . .

- A loud, repeated bark, sometimes accompanied by a growl or snarl: conveys aggression or dominance. ("Get away from here or I'll bite you!")
- Sharp, short barks: alert to intruders or danger. ("What? What? What?")
- A light, high-pitched bark: an invitation to interact or play. ("Come on out and play!")
- A low moaning-type bark: signifies anxiety. ("Who's out there?")
- Short, high-pitched yips: excitement, eagerness, friendliness, or curiosity. ("Hi! Hi! Hi!")

The Growl Says . . .

- A deep, low growl emanating from the chest and progressing to a snarl: conveys aggression. ("I'm warning you!")
- A low, assertive growl: indicates dominance. ("Get out of my yard!")
- A low, whining growl: shows worry or fear. ("*Please* don't come any closer!")
- Soft, low growling: a play signal. ("I've got the ball. See if you can take it!")

The Howl Says . . .

- A long, sustained rising howl: usually conveys fear or anxiety, as with a dog left alone. ("Where *are* you? Come back!")
- A short, happy howl: indicates an emotional greeting. ("Wow! It's great to see you!") This howl is common with northern breeds such as huskies.
- A "bay": the howl of a hound at chase ("We've spotted the fox!"); a victorious howl ("Come on! We've found it!").
- A sustained howl: in unison with the sound of a siren ("Must be something to wail about. . ."), a musical instrument (. . . or sing-along), or a choral pack response ("For we are jolly good fellows!").

The Whine Says . . .

- A long whine, rising in pitch: indicates anxiety or fear. ("I'm scared!")
- A low whine: serves as an alert. ("Listen . . . something's out there!")
- A short, worried whine: can take place during flight. ("Leave me alone, leave me alone!")
- Low, worried whining: indicates submission or subordinate rank. ("Don't hurt me. I surrender.")
- Short, eager whines: curiosity, excitement, or an invitation to play. ("Come on! I can't wait!")
- A screaming whine: used when a dog is being beaten by a dominant dog. ("Please! I can't take any more!")
- A loud, screaming whine: indicates pain or injury. ("Stop! It hurts!")

The Regional Accents of DogSpeak

Just as with human regional accents, there are as many DogSpeak accents as there are breeds. As a rule, hounds love to bay. Northern breeds such as Huskies or Malamutes get their kicks out of howling. Working dogs, with their strong sense of territory, love to bark. Terriers (as any owner knows) like to yip and yap. Toy dogs yip and whimper, while herding dogs vocalize with short, sharp barks, the perfect tool for herding sheep. And within every group and every breed, each individual dog has his own idiosyncratic sounds. Some growl for treats while others whine. Some yip at the back door to say, "Let me in!" while others whine to go out. Only by observing your own dog closely, and listening to his individual voice, can you capture his personal DogSpeak dialect.

Dogs Just Wanna Have Fun—the Language of Play

One DogSpeak communication is universal: "Let's play!" Dogs, like their wolf forbears, love to play, play, play—the more, the better. It's canine nature and it's a wonderful way for dogs to work off excess energy, learn how to socialize with other dogs, and develop a happy-go-lucky attitude that creates a good disposition. As a matter of fact, dogs kept away from other dogs tend to become aggressive, ill-tempered animals. Like wolves, dogs are naturally social creatures, which is one reason I always recommend that my clients arrange play dates with other dogs and their owners. It's a perfect way to meet new people and new dogs, and expand the social horizons of both dog and owner.

Originally, play served as a wolf training ground on which cubs learned to defend themselves and become assertive. Every bit of a wolf's play was designed to prepare the cubs for the pack lifestyle. Play taught wolf cubs to stalk their littermates in preparation for the hunt, and chasing one another was an obvious preparation for the real chase of prey. But since a wolf's lifestyle is no longer pertinent to the life of today's domestic dogs, and since your aim is to keep your dog good-natured and friendly, it's your job as the Alpha/owner to make sure play never progresses to aggression.

The most common signal that dogs use to invite play is the "play bow." Here, the dog lowers his front shoulders to the ground, leaving his rump up in the air. It's universally understood DogSpeak that says, "Come on, let's have some fun!" and it's often accompanied by excited panting. Take the challenge and you may find yourself being chased around the room, nipped at your heels, jumped on, licked, nuzzled, and nudged while your dog is barking happily, perhaps even growling a happy growl. There's no mistaking these barks and growls for aggression—not if you observe the delighted smile on your dog's face. Dogs love to chase, run, jump on you with both front feet (yes, the idea is to knock you over!), and stalk you as diligently as they might a rabbit. Dogs really just want to interact with you.

Watch two dogs at play and, if you weren't observant enough, you might believe you were watching a fight. They wrestle, take one another's muzzles in their mouths, stretch their jaws, bare their teeth, growl, yip, and roll. Even their expressions might be mistaken for expressions of dominance—lips pulled back, ears erect. But in fact, they're having the time of their lives and their happy and relaxed attitudes and body

The play bow.

language convey that. Play is a wonderful way for two canine friends to release their pent-up energies (of which they have an apparently endless supply) and to indulge in behaviors and stances that in another context could provoke hostility. Once again, it's up to you, the owner, to make absolutely certain that play never advances into aggression, since one too-hard nip could turn play into an argument and if your dog's canine friend is not well socialized, he might interpret this as a challenge and initiate a real fight. The moral here is to know your dog's best friends as well as you would your child's playmates. If you know another dog to be somewhat testy, be watchful and *never* let play escalate into something serious.

The Language of Love

Interestingly enough, the postures of play closely resemble those of courtship. The playful, somewhat infantile behavior of courtship helps the female (who is interested in knowing that her pups will have good genes) determine whether the male will be a good father to her pups. Sometimes a female will indulge in this courtship behavior for the entire period of her estrus, or heat, before allowing the male dog to mate with her.

Some of what humans often, mistakenly, interpret as courtship behavior—a dog's attempt to mount other dogs, for example—actually is more a matter of establishing dominance. That's *always* the case when male dogs mount other males, and it has no sexual connotation whatsoever. The same is true if a dog tries to mount people or children, but a dog who makes this a habit needs to be trained out of it quickly and firmly. This is *not* acceptable canine behavior, no matter how you view it.

• • •

The language called DogSpeak is complex, yet beautifully simple, and learning it will grant you closer communication with your dog than you ever believed possible. But to become fluent in DogSpeak, you must become a keen observer of your dog, every nuance of his expression, every variation of his voice, every variation of his posture, every flick of his tail. You'll find that in so doing, you'll really get to know your dog. And as with any relationship, knowing him is the first step toward creating a strong bond of friendship. And that puts you in the best possible starting position for training your dog. An aware master and attentive, well-behaved dog are, I'm sure you'll agree, the Dream Team.

Chapter 8

The Leader of the Pack

The beautiful thing about DogSpeak is that it opens up an extraordinary communication between you and your dog. Once you begin to converse with one another in this amazing language, you come closer and closer to that wonderful moment when you and your canine friend understand each other completely. Each knows, and responds to, the other's thoughts, moods, and feelings, and the two of you live and work in perfect synergy. But you can never arrive at that enviable state until you've established beyond any doubt that your dog/owner pack has a leader—*and you're it!*

Dogs, just like children, need parameters. They need (and want) clear rules, without the ambiguity that leads to conflict and, ultimately, behavior problems. They need to know that they're in the care of someone wise, someone on whom they can depend, someone they trust. It's pretty unnerving for a child *or* a dog to be dependent on someone who really isn't in control. The stronger you are, as Alpha leader, the more secure and relaxed your dog will become. Yes, dogs, just like children, will do their best to push the limits, and you, like the Alpha wolf, must maintain your authority always, with caring and compassion. The best way to do that is through obedience training.

When my clients come to me with behavior problems, I always tell them that obedience training not only can provide an immediate solution for problems, it also provides efficient new tools for communicating with your dog. As you work together in what I call "Tandem Training," your dog will develop a strong trust in you, his wise Alpha leader, and the two of you will establish an ongoing dialogue that ultimately creates an unbreakable bond of friendship. Then you move on to a brand-new relationship in which you and your dog are human/canine partners.

But suppose your dog isn't giving you problems? Why should you undertake obedience training? Here's what made one client seek out my services. Janet owned an adorable little King Charles Spaniel who, she claimed, was a perfect gentleman. He was entirely housebroken, always obedient, loving, gentle, and at her side day and night. But one day Janet discovered she was a prisoner of separation anxiety, unable to leave the house without her dog who, each time she did, howled and screamed until her neighbors were threatening to have her evicted. Fortunately, Janet called me. Her first words were, "I don't want a little robot. I want a dog with personality." I explained that obedience training is not about creating robots. It's about giving your dog the deep feeling of security that comes with having an Alpha who can be trusted. I convinced Janet that training would prove to her dog not only that it had an owner-in-charge but one that it could rely on. After just two lessons, Janet's dog was both secure and well-behaved and the separation anxiety was no longer a problem.

Now is the time to take everything you've learned about DogSpeak and put it into action. And just as you become fluent in any language by practicing it, the quickest way to become fluent in DogSpeak is to use it in training your dog. This is where you can observe, and come to know perfectly, the quirks and individual expressions that make your dog uniquely himself. If you're an observant and receptive owner, you also may find that you have much to learn from your dog. For his part, your dog will learn to interpret your signals, commands, and corrections in a language familiar to him.

Establishing Yourself as Alpha

The ideal Alpha leader gives clear messages. He's patient, persistent, and quick to praise, but when an action is inappropriate, his corrective response is swift and clear. That's a perfect description of how I train dogs. I am the Alpha, they are my obedient pack, and it's from my clear commands and equally clear corrections that we develop a single seamless unit from two very different species.

Conditioning the Behavior

Unlike humans, dogs can't grasp the human concept of right versus wrong. Their world is governed by instinct, the Eight Central Factors of Pack Behavior that are their genetic heritage and still, to a large degree, control their responses. In order for dogs to comply with the human definition of impeccable good manners, first they must be shown what that is. It's up to you, the Alpha, to explain it in DogSpeak and to make your expectations absolutely clear. In my system of training, you will learn to give a command to your dog while, using the crystal-clear body language of DogSpeak, you demonstrate to him exactly what response you want and expect. When he responds correctly, you praise him lavishly; when he doesn't, you correct him clearly and quickly. The conditioned response this technique creates is the basis for all good obedience training, and it's as crucially important to your dog as it would be to your child. It takes a lot of reminding before a child remembers to say "thank you" each time he or she receives a gift, and it's this same kind of repetition that eventually will teach your dog to be a perfect lady or gentleman, responding correctly every time you give a command.

For example, when you want your dog to sit quietly at your side, you ask him to "Sit" and accompany your command with an appropriate hand gesture and emphatic tug of the leash on the training collar. He will get the message. That's a perfect example of how DogSpeak training uses every element a dog understands—body language, simple verbal language, and leash control—to achieve the desired response. After a few repetitions, you'll find that you can eliminate the tug on the leash. Your dog will know that "Sit" means he's expected to sit. And the praise that *always* follows is his very best reward—a reward that ensures a correct response each and every time you give a command.

I know that some people reward dogs with food (they often do the same with children), but I believe that's an inappropriate use of food, creating a food-dependence that may cause obesity later in life (for dogs *and* for children). But my primary objection is that if a dog is focused on food, he isn't focused on you and so isn't learning. Worse yet, you may discover later on that he won't perform any command unless food is the reward at the end of the exercise. There are only two occasions when I use food as a reward: for puppies in the early learning stages, from eight to twenty weeks, who haven't the concentration needed to respond to training signals; and in film, stage, or television work, where a dog is required to do the same trick over and over—not because he isn't doing it right but because the director needs a different camera angle or the star wasn't on cue. In that case, I think the dog has earned a treat.

Of course, there are recalcitrant dogs—usually those of dominant nature—that just don't want to obey and rebel with the canine equivalent of a temper tantrum. Permitting such behavior effectively negates your training efforts. Any such response from your dog *must* be followed by swift correction: a sharp jerk and release of the leash against the training collar, in unison with a sharply spoken reprimand, "No!"

The only way to get the correct response—the response the command calls for—each and every time you ask, is by keeping your commands clear and your actions consistent (and consistently kind), and by giving your dog prompt praise for a job well done and equally prompt correction when it isn't. As you will see, in DogSpeak training there are four basic steps which let you achieve a perfect, positive result.

The Three P's

My motto is the Three P's—Patience, Persistence, and Praise. Patience is an essential quality for any teacher or Alpha leader. Persistence is what always results in a perfect performance. And the positive reinforcement for perfect performance *always* is praise. Even when correction is needed, it must be followed with lavish praise when the correct response finally comes. After all, your dog tried and tried again until he got it right. He's learned his lesson and now has earned his reward. I believe dogs deserve the best and I make sure each and every training session ends on a happy, upbeat note. Isn't that what you expect from your friendships.

Are Your Tools in Place?

It goes without saying that training can't begin without the proper equipment: training control collar and leash. I hope you remember the right way to use both. (If not, go back to page 71 and review the instructions.) The control collar may be metal chain links, nylon, or rolled leather, but it must be a slip collar, the sort that loosens and tightens with the tug of the leash. Otherwise, you have no control of your dog. I've seen huge dogs pulling their out-of-control owners down the street, all the while developing stronger neck muscles that let them pull even harder. A control collar nips that problem before it develops. I like to think of the training collar as a "reset button" for good behavior, which it will ensure every time.

I always recommend a six-foot leash. A leash of this length lets you walk a good six feet away from your dog while you're teaching him to remain in a Sit/Stay or Down/Stay position, and this length is especially important for when you're doing the "Come" command (which you're just about to learn).

Remember how to put the collar on correctly? (If not, look at the illustration on page 72.) Thread the links through one of the rings, then form the shape of a "P," with the loose end pointing downward on the *right* side of the dog's neck. Gravity and the weight of the chain automatically keep the collar at a comfortably loose position. If the collar doesn't loosen and tighten easily with each tug of the leash, you've probably reversed and made a "Q." Since this configuration can't loosen, it will be uncomfortable for the dog and unable to deliver your tug-telegraphic messages, which depend on the quick tightening and equally quick loosening of the collar. You're not out to choke your dog into submission, only to remind him that he's to be attentive and obedient to your commands. A quick tug-and-tighten definitely will get his attention.

Bash's Four Basic Steps of On-Leash Training

There are four basic steps involved in training your dog:

1. **Focus.** Get your dog's undivided attention.

2. **Command.** Let your body language and verbal commands tell your dog *exactly* what you expect of him.

3. **Response.** An action response from your dog that is consistent with the command given.

4. **Praise or Correction.** The reward of lavish praise when your dog has done what you ask of him; a quick, clear correction when he's refused or just hasn't understood the command, followed by praise when he finally gets it right. But when your dog doesn't get it right the first time, check yourself carefully to be sure your commands are clear and concise.

You'll see that "correction" is *not* synonymous with "punishment." That's not a word in my training vocabulary. Punishment creates a fearful dog and completely destroys any chances of a close dog/owner relationship. Correction is simply a clear corrective action that shows the behavior is not acceptable and won't be tolerated.

Step One: Focus

Within the wolf pack, all other pack members focus on the Alpha, attentively awaiting his command. Now it's up to you, the owner, to assume Alpha authority and convey your wishes to your dog in clearly articulated DogSpeak. Before you give the first training command, get your dog's complete and undivided attention focused on you and you alone. Call his name, clap your hands or your thigh, give a whistle, or make strange noises—anything that makes him prick up his ears in the now-familiar alert position that tells you, in DogSpeak, that he's listening. The presence and use of the control collar and leash will reinforce his expectation that something new and exciting is about to happen.

Now that you have his attention, the work begins.

Step Two: Command

Nature has programmed your dog to expect visual signals, the body language of the wolf pack that communicates not only your commands but your authority and reliability as well. Your dog's genetic heritage also has given him finely tuned hearing that makes him respond to clearly spoken verbal commands, the human equivalent of the Alpha wolf's short, sharp bark that says, "Follow me." Both are equally important elements in DogSpeak training.

The cardinal rule is: Keep your commands simple, short, and clear. Short, easy words such as "Heel," "Sit," and "Stay" are the basic language of obedience training. *Don't* use your dog's name; it dilutes the impact. When accompanied by reinforcing signals—an upward hand gesture for "Sit," a hand flashed before the dog's eyes for "Stay," or a pat on the thigh to accompany the word "Heel"—these words tell your dog exactly what behavior is expected of him.

Remember: Always put on a happy face. An unfailing good humor tells your dog this is fun, not punishment.

Step Three: Response

It's your simultaneous verbal command and clearly displayed gestures that get a response from your dog. Whether you get a correct or incorrect response may depend as much on you as on the dog. If your messages are mixed, your commands unclear, or your gestures muddled, don't be surprised if the dog doesn't get it. Always keep in mind the clarity of wolf language, the primal root of DogSpeak. Within the wolf pack, gestures and vocalizations are unmistakable. Your own commands and gestures must be equally easy to read so that your dog knows your intentions beyond any doubt. If he doesn't understand the command, he can't respond correctly, and his correct response always should be appropriate to your command. If you say "Sit," using the correct accompanying gestures and the right signals with the leash and collar, sit is what he *must* do. Your job is to repeat the exercise, with verbal commands and gestures, until the right response comes, always praising your dog when it does, but correcting him when it's wrong.

Step Four: Praise . . .

Praise, in my opinion, is the most important reward any dog can receive. Dogs just love to make you happy and when you shower them with praise, they know they've done their job and done it well. Besides, there's no better reinforcement tool for establishing a lifetime of perfect responsive behavior than consistent praise for a job well done. It makes your dog eager to learn more and helps him remember the lessons longer. Praise is also important in building your dog's confidence and phrases like "good dog" let him know he's done a good job.

Praise also helps establish a strong bond of trust between you and your dog. He knows that he can depend on you to reward him when he's done well, and that he can expect you to correct him carefully and gently when he's muffed the command.

. . . Or Correction Followed by Praise . . .

How *do* you correct your dog when he refuses to carry out your command? With tough love, keeping the emphasis on "love." You must establish beyond any doubt your position as Alpha leader by correcting undesirable behavior swiftly and with clear commands and gestures. Here, timing is everything. A sharp "No!" accompanied by a quick correction of the leash and collar will show your dog that his behavior was unacceptable. Repeat the command and the gestures. When your dog responds correctly, praise him lavishly, even though you may be annoyed that correction was required. Don't worry about going overboard with your praise. An abundance of love won't spoil your dog, and the strength of the praise outweighs the correction.

. . . But Never Punishment

A responsible Alpha leader *never* hits a dog. Striking a dog constitutes punishment, not correction, and far too many well-meaning people confuse the two. Hitting a dog will only make the animal "shut down" and become fearful of you and unresponsive to your commands. Even worse, it destroys the essential bond of trust that creates a strong and loving relationship between a dog and its master—the bond that lets the two of you work as a team. Striking or yelling at your dog can show him he's been "bad," *but it cannot teach him where he's gone wrong* and therefore is worthless as a teaching tool. The only thing your dog will learn from that kind of punishment is to fear you and dread the training process. The Three P's—Patience, Persistence, and Praise—are the best way to teach a dog the difference between good habits and bad.

A wise, strong Alpha leader knows how to demonstrate, through tough love, that objectionable behavior won't be tolerated but will be corrected promptly *and in a positive way.*

Basic Training Begins

Training won't get very far unless you consider your dog's point of view. That's why I developed a method of on-leash training using a DogSpeak combination of body language and verbal commands to teach dogs the ABCs of obedience. After all, the tables have turned somewhat and now your dog must learn to speak your language. It's imperative that you give him a strong background in the gestures and human language that will serve as communication between you. Just as you've learned to read the ears, the mouth, the tail, and the stance that tell you clearly what your dog is thinking, now he must focus on, and respond to, the language you call your own.

Each lesson has a highly structured form that is based on the dog's point of view and uses DogSpeak as its essential language. Each is designed to make your wishes clear through short verbal signals and body language that tell your dog, beyond doubt, what you expect of him. And each builds on the preceding one, taking your dog from the simplest obedience response to more complicated on-leash exercises. I've designed each new exercise to be done in combination with the previous lesson. It's much like the art of T'ai Chi, in which a student learns the technique one move at a time until, finally, he's working through the entire, incredibly intricate long form of this highly complicated discipline. Reviewing each lesson every time you work imprints the entire repertoire of exercises on your dog's canine consciousness, making it become a routine he does almost without effort and in an entirely relaxed and happy way. As in any discipline, repetition is the key to learning. That's why I suggest sessions of no less than ten minutes, repeated three to four times a day. (Take advantage of daily walks to practice your signals and controls, making them become an essential element of everyday life with your dog.)

Since I know that repetition without relaxation—all work and no play—does indeed make Jack a dull dog, I've developed my training method to incorporate three important elements: (1) the lesson, or command; (2) the repetition, or practice; and (3) a play session finale that always ends every lesson on an upbeat, happy note. Without the reward of play, dogs may simply shut down, as we humans do in burnout. They become bored and depressed and after a time, simply stop trying. Worse yet, they begin to view you, their teacher, not as a benevolent Alpha but as a tyrant who never lets up. It's not the best way to establish a happy dog-and-master relationship. When you remember that dogs just want to have fun (it's their wolf heritage) then you'll know that, for a dog, play is a far better reward than even the tastiest liver treat—and is far less fattening! By using game-playing after each lesson, you reinforce, in the most positive possible way, the entire repertoire of commands, helping your dog to retain the lesson and making him look forward to each new training session.

Keeping Signals Clear

The only way to train any dog successfully is to keep your signals as simple and clear as possible. When I begin training a dog, I not only combine verbal commands with body language but I use highly exaggerated gestures to dramatize those commands, making it clear to a new "student" what my command is and how I expect him to respond. Eventually, as the dog progresses from beginner to advanced pupil, he'll learn to respond to the subtlest of cues—a touch of the leash, a wiggle of the finger, a softly spoken command.

For now, the most important thing to remember is that you must make your wishes (your commands) clear to your dog, and you must do so in a calm, patient, yet authoritative manner. Now that you're Alpha, you can't afford to be tentative. Beware of giving mixed messages. Delivering a corrective "no" by smiling and saying, "Now, Charlie, you know you're not supposed to do that" will *never* get your point across. Your tone of voice, facial expression, and body gestures all must be appropriate to the verbal command given. As a matter of fact, this is a good all-around exercise for most people. I think you'll be surprised to notice how many people deliver up verbal messages that have no relation to their facial expressions. If it's something you do, here's a great opportunity not only for you to learn something about yourself (something that may be standing in the way of your getting what you want) but also to understand that DogSpeak is a language that demands clarity. No mixed messages allowed! Not in training, not in life.

Getting Started

The best place to begin training is a quiet place where there are few distractions. Later, when your dog has mastered his skills, I actually prefer more crowded, noisy areas. It helps teach your dog that his concentration must never waver from you, no matter what's going on around him. For now, however, choose an indoor spot where you have room to work, a Point A to Point B space of six to twelve feet. This will give you room to work on the Come and Sit/Stay exercises and enough space for your dog to heel. If by chance you have a very tiny dog, or a bad back that prevents stooping and leaning, you may choose to do the training exercises on a table or platform, kind of a stage on which your dog can become a stellar performer.

Here's one more reminder on how to use the control collar: Form a "P" which you slip over your dog's head, with the excess chain that makes the tail of the P falling groundward on the dog's right side. (Remember: he'll work at your left side.) Attach a six-foot training leash to begin. You're ready to work.

Attach the leash to the long end of the collar—the one directed downward—and slip your thumb through the leash's handle, closing your hand on it for security. This assures that the leash will never slip off accidentally. Now, hold the other side of the leash in your left hand, in a position that is comfortable for both you and the dog. You don't want it to choke the dog, or even be uncomfortably tight, but it must be taut enough for you to maintain control. Draw the leash across your waist, gather in the excess, and clasp it with your right hand, which should be held in a natural, comfortable position at your right side, just about belt-level. The leash should have a certain amount of "swag," but not enough to make you lose control of the dog.

(Think of it as reins for your dog.) Place the dog on your left side, the traditional stance for training. I'm often asked why left and not right. Good question! My guess is it dates back to other times, when hunters and their dogs worked as a team. Usually the hunter held his weapon in his right hand, with the dog on his left. It's a custom that's been passed down as tradition over time, much like that of mounting a horse from the left side. Now it's universal language for obedience training. Guide dogs for the blind always work on their masters' left side, as do police dogs.

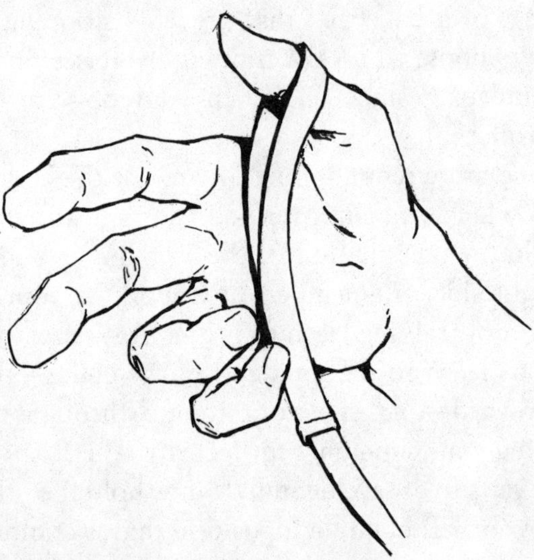

The proper way to grasp the leash handle: Hook the loop over the thumb and clasp the leash.

Now, facing an imaginary line, place your dog with his feet in line with yours. His shoulder should align with your left leg. This is a perfect starting position; DogSpeak comes next.

High-Collaring for Maximum Control

Where maximum control is required, I use the high-collar position. Here, the collar is placed directly behind the dog's ears and under its jaw, just above the throat, a position that gives total control of the dog while avoiding any gagging pressure on the throat.

High-collaring makes a dog focus on its handler—one reason it's the technique used in the show ring by handlers of champions—and with it, even a 90-pound person can control a 200-pound dog. If you want your dog to step out like a champion and be entirely obedient, try high-collaring him.

The correct high-collar position: just behind the ears and under the jaw.

Your First DogSpeak Command: "Sit"

DogSpeak is a synchronization of words, sounds, and body language. Each command, gesture, and sound must be simultaneous and clear. Since every exercise begins from a Sit position, naturally your first DogSpeak command will be "Sit." Holding the leash in your left hand, with your dog standing at your left side, gesture with an upward scooping motion of your open right hand, slightly revolving your body to face your dog. *Don't move your feet.* This is body language your dog will understand. Now, transfer the leash from your left hand to your right, using your left hand to push the dog's hindquarters into a sitting position while simultaneously pulling the leash upward to reinforce the message. (Remember, this is the early stage of training; later you won't need this additional tug of the leash or push on the rear.) Once your dog is sitting, return the leash to your left hand and flash your free right hand in front of your dog's face, while giving the command "Stay." Pause. A few-second pause lets the dog absorb this new behavior he's expected to learn. Now praise him lavishly for an exercise well done. If he didn't perform the exercise, didn't respond to your command, repeat the procedure until he does. He *will* learn, sooner than you think. By the way, keep a check on your commands to be sure they are clear enough and not conveying a confusing message.

Eventually, your dog will sit promptly and obediently from the verbal command or the gesture alone.

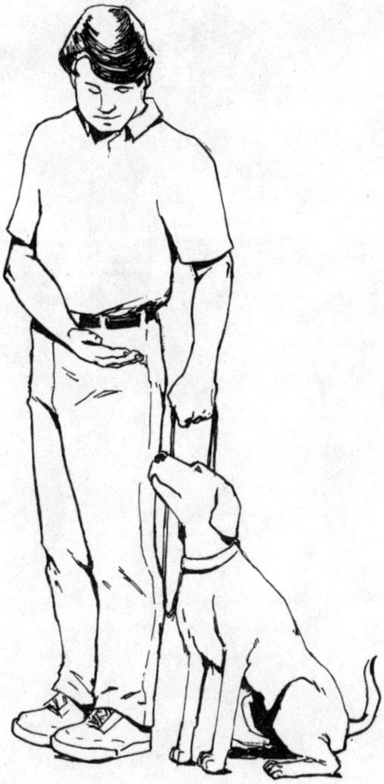

The "Sit" command, given with an upward gesture of the right hand.

Making a Correction

But what if your dog doesn't stay sitting? Prompt and clear correction is essential. If your dog gets up from his sitting position, give a sharp jerk on the leash, simultaneously saying a firm "No!" Then repeat the exercise from the beginning. Sooner or later he'll get your message. When he does the exercise correctly, praise him for a job well done.

The "Stay" command, left hand flashed in front of the dog's face.

"Stay"

Now that your dog is sitting at your side, it's important that he learn to stay until you tell him to move. Obeying the "Stay" command could save his life some day. Dropping the leash from your left hand, lean slightly forward and flash your open hand outward in front of the dog's face. This is a clear signal that says, "Don't move." Now, step forward with your *right* foot, making a half-turn to the left towards the dog. This places you directly in front of the dog, facing him. Repeating the command "Stay," step backward to half the length of the leash, or three feet from the dog. (Later you'll progress to the entire six feet.) At this point, repeat the "Stay" command and pause in position. Now walk back to your dog's right side (which places him correctly at your left), the two of you facing forward. Here comes the hard part. Pause. *Do not praise your dog yet!* Yes, I know he deserves it and I also know how proud you must be. But for a dog, praise signals the end of the training session and time to move on. *He must not move until the entire exercise is complete.*

The "Stay" command from a distance.

If He Moves

If the dog moves while you're out there at the end of the leash, *immediately* lunge forward, grabbing the leash with your right hand close to the collar and jerking it up sharply, while at the same time saying a firm "No!" This sudden exaggerated movement on your part, coupled with your no-nonsense verbal "No!," makes it clear to the dog that his action was unacceptable.

Now repeat the command to sit, make the turn, command your dog to stay, and walk backward to the end of the leash. Pause for a few moments. Return to the original Sit position, with the dog on your left side, pause for a second, and *then* praise your dog. Praise helps achieve a positive result from a negative, but necessary, correction.

Eventually you'll be able to place your dog in a Sit/Stay position and have him stay for longer periods (approximately two to five minutes).

Remember: *Always* step out with your right foot.

"Heel"

The "Heel" command tells your dog, "Walk by my side, at my pace." A well-trained dog should walk at your heel, whether the pace is quick or slow or whether you turn to left or right. Problem is, many dogs believe they're sled dogs. They pull to be out in front, which puts *them* in charge, not you. Many people make the mistake of using a harness, rather than a control collar, further exaggerating the problem. Walking a dog on a harness is like trying to control a horse with nothing more than a

The "Heel" command, given by slapping the thigh and stepping out with the left foot.

halter and a rope. The *only* way to correct a dog's pulling, which in some breeds is instinctive, is to teach the dog to heel.

To begin, place your dog in the Sit position on your left side. Now, slapping your left thigh with your hand to get the dog's attention, step forward with your *left* foot—DogSpeak body language for "move forward"—while giving a simultaneous verbal command, "Heel." The dog, with his hypersensitive peripheral vision, sees your left leg moving, feels a tug on the leash, and hears the word "Heel." It's a clear signal to him that it's time to follow the Alpha leader.

As you and the dog walk together, you should be in perfect

synch. If you aren't, it's time to exercise your right of control and think of yourself as a puppeteer or a trainer of dressage horses. Continue to give short, almost unnoticeable tugs on the leash to keep your dog in step with you. He must learn to walk *at your pace,* speeding up when you do, slowing down as your pace slows. With each short tug of the leash, you are shaping and refining his behavior, transforming him into a perfectly behaved, entirely attuned walking companion.

After you've walked a short distance, halt, and with a right-hand upward gesture, say "Sit." Give your dog only three to five seconds to respond. If he doesn't, give a short jerk of the leash, accompanied by a firm "No!" and repeat the gesture and verbal command for Sit. When the dog sits, praise him as if he'd just won the Nobel prize for good behavior.

At this point, you may follow the exercise with a "Stay" command, walk away, then come back to your dog, *pause,* and praise him. Soon you'll have your dog heeling at your side, walking at your pace without ever pulling or misbehaving. And when you come to a halt, your dog will sit automatically. Now you've not only put together a sentence in DogSpeak, but an entire paragraph.

To embellish and improve the Heel exercise, I add training behaviors such as right-about turns and left-about turns. This gives you additional mobility that's useful in crowded places. It also gives you, the Alpha, increased control over your dog's behavior, even when there are numerous distractions. No pulling, no jumping, no nonsense!

Right-About Face!

As your dog is heeling at your side, and at your pace, slap your left thigh, the signal for "Follow me no matter where I go." As you turn, swivel your left foot in an about-face, give a short tug on the leash, and say "Heel." The dog should follow right at your heel through the exercise and must pick up his pace to follow the outside of your turn. You and your dog are the human/canine equivalent of pairs skaters! Guide your dog's rhythm and pace around the turn, using the leash as your rein-in tool.

Left-About Turn

In a left-about turn, you'll turn *into* the dog. As your dog trots along in a heel position, hold your left elbow slightly back to slow the dog's pace and pivot your right foot over your left while verbally commanding "Heel." This combination of the pivoting right foot, the checking of the leash, and the verbal command "Heel" says to your dog, in DogSpeak, "We're going to make a left turn."

Now you've created an intricate dance in DogSpeak, with you and your dog perfectly attuned to one another's motion. And just as with real-life dance partners, the more you work together, the smoother the routine will become.

"Down"

The Down exercise is one of the most important in a dog's repertoire. A dog that lies quietly at his master's feet when there are visitors, or goes to his designated place on command, is a dog that is a part of the family, not an annoyance. It's easy to put a dog into the backyard when company comes, but it doesn't teach the dog how to be a part of family life without

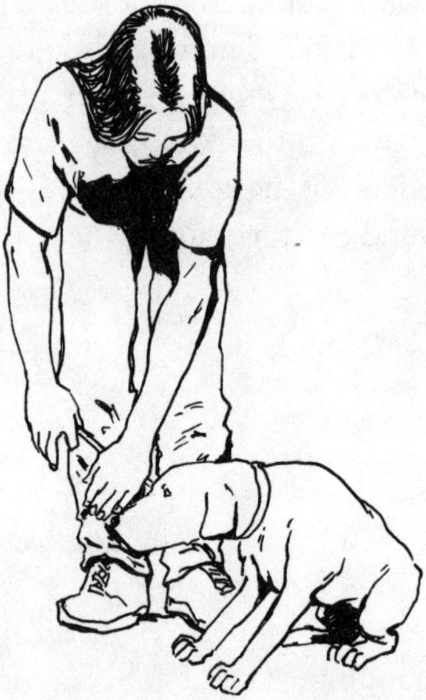

The "Down" command, gestured with the left hand.

If the dog says "No!," a slight push on his shoulders does the job.

getting in the way. All he wants to do is be with you, take part in the fun, socialize with your friends, join you on a shopping trip or be a part of the family dinner celebration. When he learns what "Down" and "Down/Stay" mean, he can! Obeying these commands is the canine equivalent of putting on "company manners," the best of doggie etiquette in action. And since your dog loves to be a part of your life, you really owe it to him to show him the behavior that will make it possible.

For now, we'll begin in a quiet place at home, with the dog sitting at your left side. Bring your right hand across to grasp the leash close to the collar. Holding the leash in your right hand, use your open left hand, palm facing downward, to pass an exaggerated downward gesture in front of the dog's eyes while you lower your own body to his eye level. (If your dog is a toy breed, you'll need to get down on one knee to perform this exercise.) Simultaneously, give the verbal command "Down" and lower the leash to apply pressure that reinforces the message. With your left hand, apply gentle pressure on the dog's shoulder to urge the dog downward. When your dog is in the correct down position, pass your left hand in front of his eyes and command him to "Stay." Pause the requisite moment, then praise him for being a great student!

If your dog really doesn't understand, or seems fearful of the exercise, grasp his front feet gently and pull them into a lying position while at the same time pushing downward on his shoulders. Remember to accompany the action with the verbal command "Down."

Always remember that, in DogSpeak, verbal commands, visual cues or gestures, and the reinforcing pressure of the leash work together to convey your wishes to your dog. He's eager to please, and if your messages are clear and direct, he will. That's why I continue to remind you that in the beginning you should keep your tone of voice firm, your gestures exaggerated, and the leash in taut control. When your dog is in perfect control, then you can relax.

The "Down/Stay" command, given with the left hand.

If Your Dog Says "No!"

If your dog is a dominant, powerful, or potentially aggressive dog, it could be dangerous to put your face close to your dog's. In this case, while giving the downward gesture with your left hand, holding the leash with your right, use your left foot to step on the leash. The pressure this creates will force the dog to the ground. He may struggle, but this is one fight you, as

Alpha, must win. When your dog finally lies as commanded, pause, then praise him to let him know you're pleased. A stubborn dog may need several repetitions of this forced Down before finally succumbing to your authority. But just like the Alpha wolf, you must fight to maintain your authority each and every day. And *you* must prevail.

"Down/Stay" from a Distance

Once your dog has learned to go down and lie quietly at your side, you can proceed to the "Down/Stay" command and walk away from your dog. With your dog in the Down position, flash your left hand before his eyes, then swivel on your right foot to face the dog, exactly as you did in the Sit/Stay exercise. Repeat the verbal command "Stay," walk backward a few feet, pause, and return to your dog. Pause again, then praise your dog for his terrific accomplishment. "What a good dog!"

The "Down/Stay" from a distance.

From "Down" to "Sit"

A good way to end this exercise is to make your dog sit from a Down position. With the dog in a Down/Stay position, slap your left thigh, the original signal for "Pay attention." As the dog looks up (thinking you're going somewhere), make an exaggerated upward gesture with your right hand, simultaneously saying "Sit" and "Stay." Pause and praise your dog with everything you've got.

To make your dog sit from a Down position, gesture upward with the right hand.

Give the command to "Sit."

Finish with the "Sit/Stay" command.

"Come"

"Come" is one of the most important words in the DogSpeak vocabulary. It brings your dog to you when you call. If, in a worst-case scenario, your leash breaks, or your dog slips out of his collar, the "Come" command will be a lifesaver. It also provides immediate control over a dominant, territorial, or aggressive dog. If someone walks onto your property unexpectedly, the "Come" command can prevent a potentially serious situation. By the way, this is the only command where I use the dog's name. That's because it's the best possible way to get his attention if he's yards away.

For the "Come" command, sweep your arm in an exaggerated gesture towards your chest.

To begin this exercise, place the dog in a Sit position and ask him to stay. Turn and walk backwards to the length of the six-foot leash, extending your left arm as it holds the leash in front of you and gesturing with your right hand for the dog to stay. Pause. Then, sweep your right arm towards your chest in an exaggerated gesture, slapping your chest while at the same time, using your dog's name, you say "Sammy! Come!" with all the excitement and enthusiasm you can muster (coming to you should sound like great fun), simultaneously pulling in the leash to reinforce the spoken command. Remember, you're the

Alpha calling the pack together. Let your voice convey enthusiasm. *Never* yell "Come over here!" at a dog, unless you want him to be afraid to come. And certainly never follow that kind of a command with an angry, "Why didn't you come when I called!" with perhaps a bit of finger-shaking thrown in for emphasis. That would make the dog view coming to you as a frightening experience, something to be avoided at all costs. Keep your cool at all times and end every command and response on a positive upbeat note.

When the dog responds correctly by coming when called, have him sit facing you, pause, then praise your dog enthusiastically. As a finale to the exercise, you'll tell the dog to "Come to Heel."

"Come to Heel"

This command tells the dog to come around your body to the left-side starting position. Holding the leash in your *right* hand, give a slight tug on the leash while simultaneously stepping back with your right foot. As the dog walks around behind you, switch the leash to your left hand. When the dog is standing in place, his shoulder in line with your leg, give the upward motion of your hand that says "Sit." Pause, then give your dog all the lavish praise he deserves for the great job he's done.

"Go to Your Place"

This command is one of the most important lessons for establishing a good working relationship with your dog. It lets you command the dog to go to his own place—his bed, his crate, any place in each room you've designated as his—and stay

Ask the dog to "Come to Heel" and bring him around your right side . . .

. . . to the correct left-side starting position.

there, out from underfoot. There's nothing more annoying than having your dog in the way while you're trying to show the plumber the leak beneath the sink, or having him jump on top of the computer repairman as he's working on a very delicate installation. Yes, you can banish the dog to his crate, but it's even better if you can tell him to banish himself. The "Go to Your Place" command tells him that, while you love his company, now is not the time for sticking his nose in the workman's business (or lunch!).

Having your dog obediently go to his own place also helps accustom him to separation, which in turn prevents development of separation anxiety, a condition stressful for both dog and owner. Just as you don't want your child climbing all over you every hour of every day, so you don't want your dog "dogging your footsteps," so to speak. You need your own quiet time, and he must learn to accept his as well. Once your dog has mastered the Down/Stay, that's easily accomplished.

Select a special place your dog likes—his bed, a corner of the room, that warm spot next to the heater. Then, with the collar and leash in position and your dog sitting or standing at your left side, command "Go to Your Place" while simultaneously pointing to that place and walking him to it at heel. Place him in a Down/Stay position and walk away. Until your dog has absorbed the command, I suggest leaving him on-leash, particularly if there are strangers in the house. If the dog moves or breaks your command, give a quick and sharp "No!," grab the leash, and lead the dog back to the same spot, giving the "Go to Your Place" followed by "Down/Stay" commands. Each time you repeat this exercise, you'll be building his expertise at staying for longer lengths of time. In the beginning, a few minutes is about it, but later on, you can expect your dog to stay for up to a half-hour. To end the exercise, return to the dog's place, have your dog sit, and then praise him lavishly for doing exactly what you asked. The "Go to Your Place" command is a great tool when you're having a family dinner or get-together and you'd like your dog to be a part of the celebration but not in the way.

Playtime

Post-session playtime lets both of you loosen up from the rigorous work of training. Both of you probably are feeling a bit tired. After all, learning a lesson and teaching one require equal concentration and are equally demanding. Relaxing and having a bit of fun will end the session happily for both of you. Being silly together, chasing and being chased, stalking each other, playing hide and seek—these are the games that are an integral part of DogSpeak and they're the very same games that wolves play with one another, each and every single day. Since such play is a vital part of wolf society, it's natural that it's equally important to the wolf's descendant, your dog. Tossing a ball or a toy for your dog to retrieve is a great release of energies that have been under tight control during the training session. Now the focus is off; the fun is on. While you're at it, you have a perfect opportunity to teach your dog to "fetch" the ball or to "drop it" at your feet. This is training without the structure, a lesson your dog won't even realize he's learning.

Play sessions also can be used to promote agility. Catching a ball mid-fly, jumping over hurdles, going through tunnels, walking a seesaw, all develop the dog's reflexes, his muscles, and his agility. Equally important, exercises such as these depend to a great degree on the dog's trust in you. If you lead him safely from one end of a seesaw to another, he knows he can rely on you not to get him into dangerous situations. At the same time, he's learning to trust his own abilities. Play of this sort is obedience in action, a joyous release of spirit that tells your dog this

Smart Games

One of the games dogs love most is hide-and-seek, a game which only should be played within a safe enclosure. In this, you tell your dog to "Sit/Stay," then hide and call your dog to "Come." This lets your dog use every one of his senses—his sense of smell, his keen hearing—to locate you. Not only does this game create closer bonding for you both, it calls on the dog's intelligence while, at the same time, it reinforces the structured lesson that has taught your dog to "Come" when called.

doing-what-I'm-told stuff is fun! And *that* is the best way to learn.

In time, as you practice and become proficient in these exercises, you'll experience a unique synergy between you and your dog—the same kind of spiritual oneness I found with my wolf, Mariah. You will have created a foundation of perfect trust and love, communication that reaches beyond the words of human language, and a spiritual bond that links the human and animal worlds in telepathic harmony.

For now, pat yourself (and your dog) on the back. You've not only put together sentences, you've had a full conversation in DogSpeak and you're ready to move on to more sophisticated matters.

Chapter 9

The Happy, Healthy Dog

Dogs are incredibly generous creatures. Their greatest joy in life is loving you, and what makes them happy is pleasing you, being with you, spending every waking and sleeping hour by your side. They will protect you with their lives, love you with their enormous hearts, and do everything in their power to make you happy. (Too bad we humans can't be more like dogs!) Keeping your dog happy is simple: Love him and fulfill his basic needs—proper care and feeding, regular walks, regular exercise, and a regular play period with you, his beloved owner. Then treat him with respect. All your dog asks in return for his devotion is your love, your compassion, and your care.

Sometimes we humans are selfish. We take our dogs' unconditional love for granted and don't give back. We may take the attitude, "Here's your food, here's your water, you've had your walk, now I'm out of here." With that treatment, a dog may still be loyal, but he certainly won't be happy. I find it difficult to comprehend how anyone could fail to return such unbounded love, which is why I always caution prospective owners to be absolutely certain of their commitment *before* they acquire a dog.

Commitment Required

Keeping a dog happy and healthy requires the same commitment that you would make to your child. But unlike your child, your dog can't voice what troubles him. He's as dependent on you as a newborn and it's up to you, his caring and compassionate owner, to hear his DogSpeak message and be there for him when he really needs help. Observing your dog, listening to him when he speaks to you, understanding his quirks of personality, and paying careful attention when something doesn't seem quite right is the responsibility of a good Alpha/owner.

For example, do his eyes look at you pleadingly and sorrowfully? Does that tell you that he may be in pain, or, at the least, extremely uncomfortable and unhappy? (If not, go back to "DogSpeak for Beginners" and brush up on your vocabulary!) Are his ears drooping in a manner that clearly tells you in DogSpeak, "I'm not a happy dog today. Something's wrong, but I don't know what it is. I need you." Is he lying on his bed, reluctant to move? Could his DogSpeak message be that it hurts to do so? Has he begun to throw up once a day? And have you considered he may have parasites, even though you've taken great pains to prevent them?

The fact is that no one, not even your vet, knows your dog as well as you do, and now that you understand DogSpeak, you'll be able to read these unmistakable signals that say your dog isn't himself. It's up to you, his Alpha/owner, to get to the root of his problem, and then help make it, and him, right again.

As You Would Have Done unto You

I've freely translated the edict "Do unto others . . ." to read "Do unto your dog as you would have done unto you." This means treating your dog to the Three C's—Compassion, Care, and Concern. All too often, well-meaning owners actually abuse their dogs without meaning to, usually through ignorance but many times through pure lack of compassion or concern. How would you like it if your joints were stiff but you were forced to walk two miles at a marathon pace? How would you feel if someone dangled you by your arms? Could you limit your bathroom visits to twice a day? Would you feel loved if you had to eat from a dirty bowl and drink stale, debris-filled water?

I've watched an unfeeling owner walking at a brisk pace while his three-legged dog gallantly struggled to keep up (still wagging his tail at simply being part of the walk). I've seen people carry their small dogs in excruciatingly uncomfortable positions, never once considering how it might feel. I've even known people who "forgot" to take their dog for its evening walk, then punished it when, unable to hold it any longer, it soiled the floor. As far as I'm concerned, an owner like that, with no compassion for his dog, doesn't deserve to have one!

But care and concern go even farther. City-dwellers who take their dogs into traffic without leashes are not only breaking the law but are showing no concern whatever for their dog's safety. (Your dog can't interpret traffic signals and he surely won't notice the car careening around the corner.) Owners who fail to inoculate their pets or take even minimal preventive care shouldn't *be* owners. If the care you give your dog doesn't equate to compassion, care, and concern, then perhaps you should have another look at your commitment.

The Healthy Dog

If you want to keep your dog healthy—and if you love him, you do—then quality care is essential. To me, that's precious little to give in return for unconditional love. However, giving your dog the best care requires close DogSpeak communication with your dog. After all, he's utterly dependent upon you. Since he has no voice himself, yours is the voice that will get him the basic care that leads to good health. He's depending on you to get him medical attention when he needs it (and he'll tell you, in clear DogSpeak, when that is), keep him vaccinated against disease, provide him with an appropriate, healthy diet, and give him regular grooming, including proper baths with the proper shampoos, and attention to details such as toenail clipping. Yes, keeping your dog healthy requires commitment. But isn't that what a loving relationship is all about?

The Relationship with Your Vet

These days, veterinary medicine is as sophisticated as human medical science. Many larger cities have medical centers equipped to do the most complicated surgery, including laser

Prescription for Healthy Teeth

Just like humans, dogs are prone to gingivitis, or gum problems. The preventive prescription is the same: regular brushing. Using either a special doggie toothbrush or a finger brush that slips over your index finger (gauze wrapped around your finger will do the trick as well) and chicken-flavored doggie toothpaste (which contains enzymes to help break down plaque), brush your dog's teeth carefully along the gum line. The process should be repeated once a week for keeping gums and teeth in good, healthy condition.

surgery, and to use state-of-the-art equipment such as MRIs and CT scans to make diagnoses that wouldn't have been possible years ago. The American Kennel Club has invested in a Health Foundation devoted to improving your dog's DNA to prevent genetic problems such as hip dysplasia. And when it comes to the latest in medications, often your four-footed friends get the newest and best long before we humans do. Once again our dogs help us by letting the medical community assess the results of these medications on their bodies before trying them on us. And you can be sure that today's veterinarian is well trained in all the newest medical techniques, from heart surgery to joint replacement. That's why your veterinarian is one of the most important people, not only in your dog's life, but in your own. He'll watch over your dog to maintain its optimum health. He'll vaccinate your dog against diseases such as rabies or parvovirus, provide you with preventive medications against dangerous parasites such as heartworm or the ticks that cause Lyme disease, and advise you on regular care, from tooth cleaning to nail clipping. He'll alert you when it's time to revaccinate and advise you when new and improved vaccines are available. He'll counsel you on your dog's special needs, from diet to shampoo, and he'll be with you as your dog grows older and his physical needs change.

Your vet also can educate and alert you to breed-specific problems such as hip dysplasia, eye problems, or skin problems, and, if necessary, can refer you to a specialist in these areas. Now there are veterinary ophthalmologists, dermatologists, gastroenterologists, cardiologists, and specialists in almost any ailment that might befall your dog. Your vet remains your greatest ally in keeping your dog healthy, and your relationship with him or her is a partnership that will endure for the life of your dog. That's why it's so supremely important to choose a veterinarian with whom you feel comfortable. The best vets listen carefully to what dog owners report. As one told me, "The owner knows his dog better than anyone, and the information he gives me can help me arrive at a correct diagnosis." Of course, it's your responsibility to report the facts calmly and objectively.

Regular veterinary checkups are crucially important. Since many preventive inoculations are due each six months, that's a perfect schedule for a thorough medical checkup in which your veterinarian will look your dog over from head to toe, checking heart, ears, teeth, coat, and skin while, at the same time, collecting any information you have to offer. Has your dog's appetite been poor lately? Now's the time to mention it. Does he seem less energetic than usual? Could be he's getting older or it could be he has a hidden problem that has an easy solution—once your vet hears about it. These preventive visits will help keep your dog in robust health. They also allow your veterinarian to develop a closer relationship with your dog and observe its special quirks and needs—useful information when it's time for a diagnosis.

Problem Health

Some dogs inherit health problems. Hip dysplasia affects a number of large breeds. Skin problems, back problems, eye problems, allergies, and acne all may be the result of genetic

Vets on the Net

The American Veterinary Medical Association has a Web site that offers complete information on your pet's health needs. Check in at:
www.avma.org/care4pets.html.

Insuring Your Dog's Future

These days, there's very little available to us that's not available to our dogs, including medical insurance. There are a great many insurance companies, with many different policies, that can ease the financial burden of a pet's serious illness. Discuss these with your vet, who is the proper person to make the right recommendation. Health insurance for your dog may be the best financial investment you ever made.

heritage. But relief is a matter of knowing how to give your dog quality of life *in spite of* his heritage, and you do that by working closely with your veterinarian.

Your veterinarian can prescribe antihistamines for nonspecific allergies, give you medicinal soaps for skin allergies, soap-free cleansers for soap allergies, special shampoos for pimples (common among terriers), and medication for sensitive stomachs. Special diets can be prescribed as well for dogs with kidney problems or digestive problems, and there are even special diets for cancer-patient dogs. Much of today's allergy medication is the same over-the-counter medication we humans use, and it can be as effective for your dog as for you. A word of warning here, however: *Never* give any medication (including your own) to your dog without your vet's clear instructions. The wrong medicine can kill!

Spaying and Neutering

Unless you plan on breeding your dog, most veterinarians believe that spaying and neutering are healthy choices. This safe procedure prevents cancer of the reproductive organs in both males and females as well as sex-linked behavior, such as aggression, urinating in the house (an extreme form of "marking" behavior), or the roaming common with unneutered male dogs. Shelters always insist that a prospective adoptive "parent" sign an agreement to spay or neuter the adopted pet within six weeks. Many people believe, erroneously, that a spayed female will gain unwanted weight. Not true. The correct caloric intake, paired with proper exercise, will keep your dog in prime condition. As for male dogs, neutering is more an affront to the owner than to the dog. It's the right choice and, you can take my word for it, your dog won't know the difference. He'll thank you, though, for the longer, healthier life ahead of him.

Coping with Serious Illness

Problems that once had only one humane solution, euthanasia, now are treated routinely and successfully with the same techniques and surgical procedures that have transformed human lives. Hip replacements are available for severe cases of hip dysplasia (that crippling genetic problem that afflicts many larger breeds); arthritis can be treated with increasingly effective medications. Recently two psychotropic drugs were approved by the FDA for use on dogs with mental problems. While I certainly don't condone drugging a dog to resolve behavior problems such as separation anxiety that are resolved easily by training, nevertheless, in seriously damaged dogs, where euthanasia is being considered, these new drugs do offer additional possibilities. Every day, new treatments are perfected to ensure that your dog need not suffer from crippling, painful, or potentially dangerous mental problems.

The Alternative Route

Not only is veterinary medicine keeping pace with modern medical science, it's branched out into alternative medicine as well, offering new approaches when traditional medicine is ineffective.

Alternative therapies are used most often in connection with chronic pain. For painful arthritis, there is the option of acupuncture or water therapy. Massage therapy may relieve the joint stiffness that comes with age. Prescribed exercise routines can encourage post-surgical healing. Homeopathic remedies often give welcome relief to a dog undergoing chemotherapy.

Before seeking alternative care, however, it's best to seek the advice of your veterinarian, who can direct you to alternative practitioners with proper credentials and a good reputation.

Acupuncture

Acupuncture is almost as old as civilization, having originated in China some 4,000 years ago. It remains the primary medicine for one-quarter of the world's population. Based on the principle of an unseen energy system, called *chi,* which flows through the body along meridians, acupuncture works on the premise that any blockage of this energy flow causes illness or disease. Acupuncturists attempt to unblock the flow by inserting needles along the correct and very precise points of this meridian that affect a given area. This supposedly releases neurotransmitters and neurohormones such as endorphins, the body's natural pain-killing hormones. As a result, the body's defense systems are stimulated and muscle spasms are lessened. According to the American Veterinary Medicine Association

(AVMA), problems such as arthritis, degenerative joint disease, certain forms of paralysis, hip dysplasia, epilepsy, and even asthma all have been treated successfully with acupuncture. It's important, of course, for you to be supportive to your dog during the treatment, which can be frightening to him. Soothe your dog, communicate in DogSpeak, and let him know that he'll be feeling much better soon. *You* are the difference between fear and faith.

Hydrotherapy

Just as hydrotherapy is receiving increased acceptance as therapy for painful human joint diseases such as arthritis, it's growing increasingly popular as a veterinary technique. Several state-of-the-art hydrotherapy centers have opened in the U.S. in recent years, offering canine patients the same restorative, pain-free therapies that have had dramatic results in their human counterparts. The veterinary results are equally dramatic: aging or diseased joints recover mobility, pain is lessened, and canine patients reap all the benefits of low-impact, stress-free exercise, from improved muscle tone to better circulation. This therapy is seen as particularly useful after surgery. While it's a delightful experience, soaking in a warmed pool, your dog may be nervous when he finds himself on the edge of all that water. Here's where you can help soothe him by talking to him in a calm voice, by telling him that everything (including him) will be fine, by letting him know that you're there, standing by.

Chiropractic

Chiropractic treatment for humans has been available in the United States since 1895, though the technique has been documented as far back as ancient China. In fact, it's even referred to in the writings of the Egyptians and Hippocrates. Chiropractic medicine concerns the relationship of the nervous system to the spinal column and musculoskeletal structure of the body. Chiropractors believe that abnormal tensions on the vertebrae of the spinal column create physiological misalignments that negatively impact nerve function. The most common consequences of misalignment are pain and loss of performance, though many believe that organ function and immune responses may be affected as well, since nerves originating in the spinal cord impact organs in the body. While chiropractic remains a relatively new technique in veterinary care, it is receiving increased attention as a potential tool for treating animals with problems such as hip dysplasia, stiffness in joints, or even loss of mobility. And while chiropractic has not been endorsed officially by the AVMA, many veterinarians recommend it. Once again, discuss all the possibilities with your own vet. If you decide to try chiropractic, go along with your dog for the treatment. This time he probably *won't* be nervous. The manipulation feels good and he'll no doubt relax into it. Nevertheless, it's important that you be there to reassure him and let him know that you approve of his being in someone else's capable hands.

Homeopathy

Homeopathy was founded in Germany in the early 1800s and is a system of therapeutics based on the principle that a disease or ailment can be treated by administering small doses of a remedy that would produce clinical signs similar to the disease being treated. In homeopathic theory, the body thus is encouraged to build up its own immune system to combat the problem. Most homeopathic remedies are made from plants; some are animal or mineral extracts that are diluted to infinitesimal amounts, then placed in a capsule or tablet made palatable to dogs. Though the scientific community remains skeptical, the AVMA asserts that medical results from such treatments frequently are spectacular, especially in cases where conventional medicine has failed. In one reported case, an accidentally poisoned dog suffered seizures and hemorrhaging. Veterinarians were able to control the seizures with drugs for some time, but when a homeopathic remedy was administered the hemorrhaging stopped. A second, later dose stopped seizures within five minutes and the dog made a full recovery.

Though homeopathy remains something of an unknown entity, with results like these, it's worth discussing with your own vet.

Nutraceuticals

Nutraceuticals are dietary supplements designed to treat or prevent disease, though FDA regulations prohibit manufacturers from making any such claims. Nutraceuticals include such substances as omega-3 fatty acids to reduce inflammations, enzymes for gastrointestinal upsets, and antioxidants for cancer prevention. These are the same sorts of products marketed to health-conscious humans by health-food and vitamin shops, and their growing popularity proves once more the pet owner's desire to provide state-of-the-art care for man's best friend. Shark cartilage, for example, has achieved remarkable results in the treatment of severe arthritis and inflammation of the joints in dogs—so remarkable, in fact, that the medical establishment now is doing additional research on shark cartilage and its efficacy in the treatment of human arthritic conditions. Once again, our four-legged friends are serving as scouts in the front lines of medical breakthroughs. Nutraceuticals are available in pet-supply stores or on the Internet. But *please don't order* until you've discussed them with your vet! And while you're at it, ask him what he thinks about vitamins for your dog as part of its daily routine.

Massage Therapy

Almost everyone loves a good massage, and your dog is no exception. Massage therapy, done correctly, can loosen tight muscles, calm tense nerves, and lessen the pain that comes with aging joints. Best of all, massage therapy is one technique that *you* can perform on your pet. I've watched a wired, high-strung dog become as mellow as a marshmallow under the soothing touch of a calming, controlled massage. Massage is an ideal therapy for overactive dogs, for overweight dogs who don't like to walk (it stimulates the circulatory system), for dogs with arthritic conditions, and for dogs that are recovering from surgery. Aside from its therapeutic benefits, the tactile experience of massage reinforces the bond between dog and owner, or caretaker, and creates the trust that, in DogSpeak, says "I'm glad we're family."

Bash's Magic Massage

Here's a quick course in how to give my magical therapeutic massage to your dog:

- Begin at your dog's head, using your thumbs to massage the skull, firmly but gently and soothingly, beginning at the indentation between the eyes. Work your thumbs in a circular motion, from that point back to behind the ears. Massage the ears between thumb and forefinger, working upward on prick ears, downward on flop ears.

- Now, place your thumbs behind the ears and your fingers along the cheekbones, using a circular motion to massage the jawbone and glands. Take care! If the dog has an ear problem, it may be quite sensitive in this area, a sure alert to you that you should take your dog to the vet to have its ears checked.
- Beginning at the back of your dog's neck, on the spine, use your thumbs as a focal point and work downward in a slightly circular motion along the shoulder blades and down the legs, one at a time, to the elbows, then the toes. Be sure to massage each individual toe.
- Now work your way down the spine to the hips and, one leg at a time, work downward to the hocks, then to the paws and toe joints, massaging firmly all the while. If your dog isn't already asleep (or even if he is), take his tail between your thumb and forefinger and massage each and every joint, from tailbone to tip.

If you'll check out your dog's post-massage contented expression—ears drooping, eyes half-closed, body completely relaxed—you probably won't miss the DogSpeak message: "This is bliss!"

A Healthy Diet

In today's saturated marketplace, there are so many different types of dog foods that the average dog owner often feels overwhelmed. It's difficult for a layman to make an intelligent choice. Do you want dry food or moist? Special diet or grocery-store special? And—this one's important—how much of it do you give? And how often?

No one is better qualified to make a dietary recommendation than your veterinarian. Today's veterinarians have a far-flung network that lets them stay in touch with specialists in the field of gastroenterology and keeps them updated as to new products and new nutritional information as it surfaces. Your vet is the person who will recommend the appropriate balanced diet for your dog, and tell you how much to feed and when to feed, based on your dog's age, breed, and physical idiosyncrasies. Today's foods are carefully formulated to provide proper nutrition and carefully monitored calories. Under

No Dogs at the Table

I strongly disapprove of feeding dogs tidbits at the table. For one thing, it creates a dog who begs and becomes a nuisance. What he's never tasted can't entice him. Besides, table scraps aren't the best nutritional choice for your dog, and some "people food" is downright dangerous. Did you know that chocolate is highly toxic to a dog? Spicy foods, as tempting to dogs as to humans, are irritating to dogs' digestive systems. Ask your veterinarian which human foods might be harmful, and *keep these foods away from your pet.* His digestive system is very different from yours, and far more sensitive, so don't assume that what tastes good is also "good for." You may end up with a gastrointestinal nightmare—one you'll have to clean up!

normal circumstances, they are designed to keep dogs of all ages in optimum health. But suppose your dog has a sensitive stomach, kidney problems, or even food allergies? Then one of the myriad special diets may be in order. Again, your veterinarian is the one to prescribe and, in some cases, even provide the special food.

Since a common failing among dog owners is rewarding an adorable, beloved companion with food treats, regular medical checkups will let your vet spot potential weight problems. He knows that overweight *isn't* healthy and he'll be quick to point out if your dog has lost his waistline. And just in case you didn't know your dog *had* a waistline, here's how you can check it for yourself: Look at your dog from above (not from a side view). A dog's waistline is just below his rib cage. If he has an hourglass figure, with a definite indentation below the ribs and before the hindquarters, he's in great shape. If it's a straight line from there to here, time to put Fido on a diet! There are special "light" foods for that as well.

A Safe Place

Dogs, just like toddlers, can be their own worst enemies. Dogs' genetic makeup imprints them with the exploratory behavior of wolves, which means they'll investigate anything, chew anything, eat anything, and get into everything they shouldn't. Just like toddlers, dogs need a safe environment, and that's your responsibility as owner and Alpha. It's for this reason that I always recommend crates and pressure gates for confining young pups who can't resist getting into trouble in their explorations. There are countless objects, plants, and foods in every household that can be detrimental to your dog's health, some even fatal. Many plants, such as holly or mistletoe, even common household plants like philodendron, are poisonous to dogs. So are bulbs, such as hyacinths or daffodils, so if you're storing bulbs in your basement, beware! Cleaning products, all poisonous to dogs, should be kept locked, just as they would be if there were a toddler in the house. So should pesticides. And there's a hidden killer in your garage—antifreeze! With its delicious sweet taste, it's irresistible to your dog. It's also deadly.

If your dog chews on a light cord, he's in danger of electrocution. Even the garbage can, which may contain tasty morsels such as chicken bones, can be dangerous turf for a dog whose only concern is how good it tastes, not whether it can shred and perforate his intestines. (For the record, *always* dispose of chicken bones immediately and outside of the house!) And an overdose of chocolate can kill a dog.

Surprisingly, some common treats, such as rawhide strips, can be dangerous as well to dogs with delicate digestive systems. Your vet is the right person to consult as to what treats are safe for your dog. Even toys aren't puppy-proof and many a dog owner has discovered, to his dismay, that the dog has eaten the tennis ball. All too often, painful and expensive surgery is

Chocolates and Dogs: Fatal Attraction

Of all the potentially harmful substances to which a dog is exposed on a regular basis, chocolate is the most dangerous. It contains theobromine and caffeine, two substances which affect both the heart and the nervous system. An overdose of chocolates can be fatal to your dog! Keep them safely out of reach, and caution your kids against ever sharing their chocolates with the pup. Not even a lick of chocolate ice cream.

the result. It's helpful to remember that dogs, especially puppies, are as inquisitive as toddlers, and need to be protected from their own insatiable curiosity.

The Well-Groomed Dog

Whether you do it yourself or have it done professionally, regular grooming is essential to the well-being of your dog. A well-groomed dog is a comfortable dog and a comfortable dog, as a rule, is a happy one. If you've never noticed how proud your dog is when he knows he's looking his best . . . well, you better begin brushing up on your DogSpeak vocabulary! Dogs, just like people, know when they're looking good, and are embarrassed when they're not. I know a little poodle who got a terrible haircut and hid under a chair for days until her hair began to grow back. Yes, even dogs hate bad hair days.

But regular grooming is important for reasons other than appearance. It serves both as flea control and odor control (important when the dog is living in the house), and it keeps your dog's coat free of mats and in top-notch condition. Since flea allergies can cause serious skin problems and ticks can infect a dog (and its family) with Lyme disease, regular baths are essential to good health.

I recommend once-a-month grooming for keeping your dog looking and feeling his best. If you choose to do the job yourself, you'll find countless products to work with, from shampoos to clippers. (You'll also read about my Home Spa Beauty Bath on page 198.) But beware: I know a famous hair stylist who decided to take his clippers to his own dog. By the time he'd finished trying to even out the dog's coat, the dog was shaved!

If you opt for professional grooming (something I heartily

recommend for oversized breeds or dogs with thick or long coats), your groomer can be one of your best allies. Of course, it's important to find a groomer who's a good temperament match, both for your dog and for you—someone who is calm and patient with your pet, attentive and responsive to you and your instructions. After all, you have a right to say how you think your dog looks best.

In the past, it was thought that too-frequent bathing was detrimental to a dog's skin and coat. That was true then, when dog shampoos were harsh and detergent-loaded. Nowadays, canine shampoos and products are as state-of-the-art as those you use on your own hair. Most are specially formulated to prevent drying, many are medicated and designed to solve special problems such as skin allergies (including flea allergies, dermatitis, or the acne common to certain breeds such as Schnauzers). Again, when it comes to skin problems, your veterinarian is the one to prescribe; your groomer will cooperate by following his instructions to the letter.

One of the advantages of regular grooming is that it presents the perfect opportunity for cleaning your dog's ears and clipping his nails. In former times, less-frequent bathing (which meant less frequent attention to the ears and nails) contributed to annoying and painful ear infections and nails that grew too long and caused pain on walking or bled when they broke. With monthly grooming more or less the norm now, more regular attention to ears and nails helps keep your dog comfortable, healthy, happy, and beautiful. Yes, a healthy dog is a happy dog, but a healthy *and* beautifully groomed dog is one proud animal!

While monthly grooming is ideal, in some cases, particularly with longhaired breeds whose coats may become matted, it's necessary to groom twice monthly. And if there are members of the canine/owner pack who have allergies, weekly baths may become necessary to reduce dander. Your vet and your allergist are most qualified to advise on this.

Between grooming sessions, there's regular maintenance. This means a regular, sometimes daily, routine of brushing, combing, and touching your dog. (Detailed, how-to instructions follow.) Obviously longhaired breeds will require more frequent brushing than, say, a shorthaired dog like a Jack Russell terrier. Since most dogs like being fussed over, this tactile experience serves to strengthen the pack bond between you and your pet. It's precisely what wolves do within the pack to convey "You're one of us and we love you." Just check out the blissful expression in your dog's eyes, his relaxed body, his half-mast ears, and you'll have the perfect DogSpeak articulation of happiness.

The Daily Brush-Out

First things first. You need to replace the Starter Kit comb and brush with the right comb and brush for your adult dog. Different breed coats require different grooming tools, and your professional groomer can make the best recommendation for your particular dog. For longhaired breeds, I recommend a "coarse comb," a wide-toothed metal comb. This lets you separate any matted hair, particularly around the sensitive head and ear areas. The brush should be what is known as a "slicker brush," a metal-bristle brush that can get through the thickest coat to remove matting and achieve a slick coat. There are numerous styles of slicker brushes. Again, your dog's groomer will give you the right brush for your dog's coat.

Mats, by the way, can be extremely uncomfortable, even painful, to your dog, which is why regular grooming is essential for keeping your dog mat-free and beautifully groomed.

Buying the Best Brush for Your Breed

With the enormous choice of brushes and grooming tools available, it's easy to be overwhelmed. Here are some quick guidelines for buying the right tools for your breed:

Shorthair Breeds (Jack Russells, Dachshunds, Boston Terriers)

- Rubber curry brush or glove brush for removing dead hair

Longhair Breeds (Tibetan Terriers, Afghans, Bearded Collies)

- Pin brush, for daily brushing
- Curved slicker brush, for working through tangles
- Coarse comb

Wirehaired Breeds (Schnauzers, Wire-Hair Fox Terriers)

- Straight slicker brush
- Double-sided metal comb, with fine teeth used for eye area, coarse for the body

Double-Coated Breeds (Shepherds, Malamutes, Chows, Huskies)

- Undercoat rake
- Straight slicker brush
- Coarse comb

Curly-Coated Breeds (Portuguese Water Dogs, Bichon Frises, Poodles)

- Curved slicker brush
- Double-sided metal comb

Of course, dogs, just like kids, hate having their hair brushed if it's painful. (You would too!) That's why it's your responsibility to acquire the skills that will let you give your dog a *comfortable* home-grooming session. Here are some tips on accustoming your dog to the experience, and brushing him out the pain-free way.

- Some dogs shy away from unfamiliar objects (saying in DogSpeak, "I'm not going closer till I check this out"), and the brush qualifies. First let your dog examine the brush by placing it on the floor for his "sniff test." Then pick up the brush and let him continue sniffing it in your hand.
- Place a leash on your dog (it serves as a security blanket) and, when possible, place your dog on a counter or table where he's less likely to try to escape. A grooming table is ideal (and, at around $50, an inexpensive aid). If that's impractical, ask a family member or friend to hold the dog for you while you groom. This gives the dog double reassurance. Another solution is a suction attachment with a "noose" for holding your dog's head. This is similar to the professional equipment used by groomers; the suction cup lets you attach it to a cabinet door or wall above your table. Or you can purchase a portable arm and noose to attach to your grooming surface. These tools can be purchased at pet-supply houses or through pet catalogs and the Internet.
- Before you begin the actual brushing, start by stroking your dog's body gently, from his head to the tip of his tail. Talk to him in a soothing voice and reassure him that this is going to feel good. Then begin to comb him with your fingertips and, afterward, fingernails. This will accustom a fearful dog to the experience of being brushed. After the finger-combing session, tell your dog what a great pal he is and give him a treat. Something wonderful, like dried liver.

- The next grooming session, repeat the performance by once again showing your dog the brush and letting him sniff it to get reacquainted. Then place him on the table and repeat the finger-grooming process. What's he saying in DogSpeak? Are his eyes bright, body relaxed, tail straight out? He's undoubtedly saying, "I'm a happy dog." Now bring out the brush and let him sniff it once again. Begin brushing your dog *very gently,* starting at his back and sides, working from his neck down to his tail. For now, brush your dog's coat in the same direction as its growth, which will diminish any pulling. By all means, continue to speak soothingly to your dog and tell him what a good dog he is. Gently continue brushing until you've worked your way over every inch of your dog—*except* his more sensitive parts, such as his face (particularly the eye area and muzzle), his ears, or his belly. That's where you'll use the coarse comb.
- With the comb, *gently* comb your dog's hair back away from his eyes, taking extreme care not to get close to the eyes themselves. It's important to support your dog's hair with your hand, to avoid painful pulling—just as you do with your own hair when you're trying to comb out a nasty tangle. Then place your hand beneath your dog's muzzle for support and comb gently, first one side, then the other. Continue to speak to your dog soothingly, in a calming voice. The tail, which generally has coarser hair, should be brushed out first with the slicker, then combed, then brushed a second time, always working from the base of the tail to the tip to create a beautiful, full plume.

Remember, when it comes to brushing and combing, it's important to be firm. *Don't* give in if your dog says, "I'm not going to let you touch me!" Be insistent, be gentle, be soothing, and be in control. You are the Alpha, after all. If your dog growls or tries to dominate the situation, grab his collar, put your hand firmly over his muzzle, and say, "No! Stop it!" You'll nip a bad situation in the bud before it gets out of hand, and you'll retain your Alpha status. Remember, timing is essential, and reprimands must be immediate, crystal clear, and *firm*.

The Home Spa Beauty Bath

Some dogs require bathing more frequently than grooming. In that case, you're the substitute bath master, and whether your dog is large or small will determine how and where you bathe him. The bathtub is the usual place; for toy breeds, you could even use the kitchen sink. It's always useful to have a spray hose attachment, which will help assure that all shampoo is thoroughly rinsed, and it's imperative to have a rubber bath mat to give your dog a feeling of security and prevent him from slipping and sliding in soapy water. The same suction attachments and nooses you used for grooming are equally handy for baths, letting you secure your dog so that he doesn't jump around or leap from the tub, and leaving both of your hands free for the job.

Picking the Product

Pet shampoos today are every bit as scientifically formulated as those you use on your own hair. There are shampoos for puppies, shampoos for sensitive skin, shampoos for skin problems, shampoos for whitening, and shampoos designed to kill fleas and ticks. There are even conditioners and rinses to add gloss to the coat and prevent matting. Your groomer and your vet are best qualified to choose the right shampoo for your special dog.

Preparing Your Pet

Before you bathe your dog at home, always do as your professional groomer does and brush him out thoroughly. This gets rid of tangles and mats that will get even worse once the water hits them, leaving you with a grooming job that's even more difficult, and possibly painful for your pet. (Naturally, you'll give your dog a final beauty-brushing once he's clean and dry.)

Water in your dog's ears can cause infections and discomfort, which is why groomers always insert cotton into the ear canals before bathing. This protects sensitive ears and eliminates the possibility of your dog's developing "swimmer's ear." (Just don't forget to remove the cotton when the bath is done. If your dog is shaking his head inexplicably, or refusing to come when called, he's telling you in unmistakable DogSpeak that you've left the cotton in his ears.) Bath time is a good time for ear-cleaning, so before you insert the cotton, clean your dog's ears by using a professional ear-cleaning product, which your veterinarian will provide. Usually this comes in a squirt bottle, which lets you flush the dog's ears. Massage them gently, then clean out the residue with a cotton ball. Ask your vet or groomer to show you the correct technique. By using it, your dog will never be the victim of ear infections.

As we all know, soap in the eyes hurts, and is as unpleasant for your dog as for you. There are petroleum lubricants your vet can supply which will coat the eyes and protect them from any shampoo irritation. This simple precaution will make the bath experience far less traumatic for your pet and will lessen the chances of serious irritation.

Before you put your dog into the tub, *test the water.* And remember that your hands are more accustomed to hot water than your dog's sensitive skin. Warm is the best temperature, for dogs just as for babies. Bathing your dog outdoors with the garden hose is fine and refreshing in hot weather (that means 85°F and higher). But doing so in cool or cold weather is torturous for your dog, just as it would be for you.

Exercise

A carefully planned exercise regimen is as important for your dog's health as it is for your own. For both of you, it builds muscle, strengthens bones, increases lung capacity, strengthens the heart, improves circulation, and produces endorphins, the "pleasure hormone" that contributes to a sense of well-being and relaxation. With benefits like that, who wouldn't exercise? Neither humans nor dogs, it turns out, without a certain amount of prodding. Dogs become couch potatoes as quickly as their masters and they won't exercise unless it's fun. That's why exercising together is the perfect answer for owner and dog . . . and a lot more fun than a solitary workout.

Just as you wouldn't (I hope!) embark on a strenuous exercise regimen without first having a medical checkup, so you won't prescribe it for your dog. Your veterinarian is best qualified to tell you how much your dog can do, and for how long. Small breeds have different requirements from large dogs; age also enters into the exercise equation. If you're both young and fit, then a vigorous run, a bike ride, a thirty-minute Frisbee session, or a mile-long power walk will give each of you the requisite exercise. But what happens if you're young and fit but your dog is mature and beginning to show it? Your dog can join you in a long walk (though if he shows signs of exhaustion, or seems stiff or in pain, head for home), and can sit and watch while you lob a tennis ball or practice your golf swing. And if the shoe is on the other foot—your dog is young and active and you're feeling the aches and pains of middle age—then there are numerous "fetch" games that let you take it easy while your dog gets the vigorous exercise.

High-Tech Exercise

Treadmills are a terrific exercise solution for both dogs and people, and I've watched the pounds melt off overweight dogs once they've been put on a regular treadmill routine. Besides, it's a great exercise option when the weather outside is frightful. You'll find these treadmills advertised in dog-related magazines and in dog-supply catalogs.

One word of caution: *Never* ask your dog to exercise vigorously in hot weather. Your dog's normal temperature is 102 degrees, which makes him far more susceptible to heat stroke than you are. I often see unthinking owners having their dogs run beside their bicycles on hot summer days, as the poor dog pants and struggles to keep up. This not only is careless, it's *inhumane*. Even asking a small dog (whose short legs can't begin to keep up with your long strides) to walk at your pace is not the action of a compassionate and loving Alpha.

In the Doghouse

I really don't approve of leaving dogs outside unattended. Left alone for long periods of time, they may become problem barkers, creating ill will with your neighbors. Even professional kennels don't leave dogs outside all the time. Instead, they have runs where dogs can go outdoors, returning to their indoor dens at will. However, if you do leave your dog outdoors, in a safe enclosure, it's essential that you provide it with proper housing. That means a doghouse that is waterproof, properly insulated against cold and heat, situated under the shade of a tree, built off the ground to prevent moisture seepage, and furnished with warm, flea-resistant bedding. Make sure there's plenty of fresh water available. (And remember also that fresh water freezes in cold weather!)

Frankly, I don't think any dog should be asked to stay outdoors in severe weather, cold *or* hot. The best housing is your house and that's where the four-legged member of your family belongs. On really cold nights, a 102-degree dog snuggling next to you, or even on the floor next to your bed, can generate plenty of cozy heat. (That's how "three-dog night" became part of the language!) And if you disapprove of dog hair on the sofa, then how about transforming that basement family room into the family-pet room? Don't you think he deserves at least that?

Safety First

Often we endanger our pets without even realizing it. Believing that a dog outside is happier than one just sitting around the house (a fallacy, since he's always happier with you), some dog owners tie their dogs on clotheslines, expecting the dog to exercise itself. First of all, he won't. He'll sit there, feeling abandoned. But tying your dog outside, unless you're around to watch over him, is a dangerous game. He may become tangled around a tree or a pole and choke to death. And if he's attacked by another intruder dog, he has no way to protect himself.

I'm equally adamant about tying a dog in front of a shop or

supermarket while you are inside shopping. These days, you may come out and discover he's been "dognapped." Sad to say, the fate of a dog that's been grabbed usually is tragic.

Happy, Happy!

A healthy dog has a head-start on happy—*mens sano en cane sano*—and a dog that feels good, has a bounce in his step, is energetic, alert, and ready to go wherever you lead is already an optimistic dog. And this is where you, the Alpha, enter this equation. Much of your dog's happiness (and consequently, his health) depends on your response to him. Your dog wants nothing more than to please you. But if what he gets instead is anger, constant reprimands, or even complete lack of attention, his naturally upbeat nature will turn to depression, apathy, anxiety, and, finally, illness. Knowing the dog's natural desire to do his master's bidding, I find it difficult to understand how anyone could not respond in kind. Dogs are such wonderful, warm, and loving creatures who tell you, each and every day, in clear DogSpeak, how they love you, appreciate you, and want to be with you. That sort of adoration is pretty hard to resist.

Dogs are social creatures and need social interaction, both from humans and other dogs. Dogs also are hard-wired for play, and without it they grow dull and listless. If you have committed yourself to ownership of one of these incredible creatures, you also have committed yourself to spending *at least thirty minutes each day* giving your dog your undivided attention. Most dog owners are passionate about their pets and want to spend time with them, but in our hectic times, many are overworked, overstretched, and overtense, and when they come home from work they're often too tired for a game. It's time to take a long, hard look at that problem, both for the health of your dog and your own. When your dog greets you excitedly at the door, bright-eyed, tail wagging wildly, welcoming you with all the love in his heart, *please* respond in kind! It's his DogSpeak message that he's excited to see you and glad you're home. The ball he drops at your feet will tell you he needs to play. When you flop into your easy chair and switch on the television, his drooping ears and the forlorn look in his eyes say clearly in DogSpeak, "I'm so sad." And when that happens, please remind yourself of your commitment and give your dog a few minutes of well-deserved and undivided attention. My bet is that you both will begin to perk up and you may find there's plenty of time and energy for a quick game of fetch. I'll guarantee it will do wonders for your own psyche as well as for your dog's. Dogs, just like people, need love, attention, and approval. Without it, just like people, they simply give up and lapse into serious depression. Fortunately, dogs are experts at asking for what they need, and a wise Alpha will know how to listen and respond.

The Sunset Years

You and your dog have been together for twelve years now. He's stood by you through the good times and the bad, and you can't imagine life without him. And yet, much as you don't want to admit it, you see he's slowing down. Some of the time he tells you he just doesn't feel up to a romp. He sleeps more, and when he gets up, it's easy to see how difficult it is for him to get going. His walk is stiff, his muzzle definitely graying. Yes, he's getting old. The games you used to play . . . well, he can't see the ball so well anymore and when you call him, sometimes he just doesn't hear you. But through it all, he wags his tail and tells you in DogSpeak that he's still there for you—he's just not as spry as he once was.

For you, it's difficult to accept that he isn't the same dog that chased you around the yard, raced after squirrels, gamboled through the fields, and cooled off by diving into the pond. And you begin to dread that inevitable day when he won't be with you any more. All the more reason to prepare for it and, even more important, to prepare for his changing needs.

Getting old isn't a picnic, for dogs or humans, but there is a great deal you can do to ease the transition. You can change your habits to accommodate the aching joints, you can provide a diet that's easier on his less robust digestion, and you can give him a bed that makes the arthritic pains of old age more tolerable. Most of all, you can be there for him when he needs you.

Most dogs begin to slow down at around ten years of age. Of course, this varies with the size of the dog. Larger dogs age far more rapidly and have a shorter life expectancy than smaller breeds. For example, Irish Wolfhounds live only from six to ten years, while Chihuahuas may live anywhere from eighteen to twenty-one years.

The first sign of age is the graying of the muzzle, followed by a certain stiffness. It's the middle-age osteoarthritis that affects most of us humans as well, beginning in our mid-forties. As the aging process continues, vision and hearing are affected. You may find your dog ignoring other dogs where once he was outgoing and friendly. Could be he doesn't see them. Or perhaps he doesn't come when you call him or bark when the doorbell rings. More likely than not, his hearing's going. Old age comes to dogs exactly as it does to people, one problem at a time. And before you've even realized it, your dog is old.

If he's healthy, then you're very lucky indeed. But this is the stage when difficult problems begin and the older dog reverts to puppy problems—inability to control the bladder or the bowels. In addition, there may be a loss of appetite, a new irritability, lethargy. The immune system begins to break down, causing respiratory problems, kidney problems, or heart problems. Glaucoma may develop. It's now that you'll need to begin seeing your dog in another light, and caring for him as you did when he was just a pup.

Now is when compassion is of supreme importance. If you're young and vigorous, putting yourself in his place may not be so easy. (If you're a senior yourself, you'll know just how he's feeling!) But do try to understand that he still wants to do everything you once did together . . . he just can't. However, there are things you can do to improve his general state of health, and to make him as comfortable as possible.

Quality nutrition is essential at this stage of your dog's life. Most top-flight dog-food companies make special food for older dogs, designed to cause less stress on the digestive system while providing optimum nutrition, greater roughage, and fewer calories for a dog that no longer can exercise as he once did. Your vet may prescribe vitamins with high levels of omega-3 fatty acids, those amino acids which pump up the immune system and keep the coat glossy and the eyes clear. Other supplements, such as shark or bovine cartilage, may be added to combat the aches and pains of arthritis. In severe cases, your vet may prescribe anti-inflammatory drugs to prevent swelling of the joints, or homeopathic remedies. He also may recommend some form of alternative care such as acupuncture or hydrotherapy. Pet-supply shops can provide you with special bedding for aging joints, the same egg-crate foam routinely used in hospitals for human patients undergoing joint replacement.

There may be an onset of diabetes, a disease common to older dogs. Your vet may prescribe regular insulin injections, special diets, or other medications designed to keep the problem under control. And you must learn to be vigilant for any signs of further deterioration, reporting them immediately to your veterinarian.

Just as with people, teeth begin to go. If you've taken good care of your dog's teeth, with regular brushing and regular dental checkups at your vet, his teeth may outlast him, but chances are that if he lives to a very old age, he'll lose quite a few of them. You'll need to adjust his diet to food he can eat. Here again, your vet is the person to advise you. As a result of his tooth problems, your dog may develop bad breath. You can combat this by using a special doggie dental paste which you apply to his gums with your finger.

As aging proceeds, it's a sad thing to see your beloved pet lose control of his bladder or his bowels, and it's far more embarrassing for him than for you. He's been housebroken all his life; now he's messed on the rug. He's devastated. If you're furious, that only compounds his psychological pain. Please, whatever you do, *don't* chastise an older dog for accidents he just can't help. Be compassionate, be kind, be understanding, and, above all, be reassuring. Let him know that this won't come between you, that you'll love him to the end. After giving you a lifetime of love, he deserves that much.

Instead of getting angry, go back to those things you did when he was just a pup. Shorten the time between bathroom walks, and don't begrudge him the extra time. If his system really is going down and he's soiling the house regularly, you may need to put down papers, to "puppy-proof" the house once more. In fact, you may need to go back to confining him in his own "room," where the floors are moisture-proofed (with plastic beneath the paper, remember?) and the pressure gate keeps him from turning the house into a bathroom. You will need to keep reminding yourself that this is what happens in old age, both to pets and to people. Always remember the good old days and be compassionate. He's not the dog he once was.

When Walks Are a Problem

When your dog just can't take that long walk he's so accustomed to, and it breaks both your hearts for him to stay home, a shopping cart fitted out with a pillow is a simple alternative. I've seen people use everything from a baby stroller to a Flexible Flyer wagon. It's a great way to let him accompany you on your comings and goings, just like the good old days. But do be sure your dog is secure. A tumble onto the sidewalk would *not* be good.

When your dog is old and infirm, what he needs most is rest. Don't ask him to do more than he tells you he can. On the days he's feeling good, his bright eyes, erect body, and happily wagging tail will tell you in DogSpeak that he's up to a walk today. But if a half-hearted flip of his tail and a forlorn look in his eyes delivers the DogSpeak message, "I think I'll just hang out here and wait for you," don't insist. He just can't.

Your dog's sunset years are a good time for the entire family to learn more about responsible pet ownership. It's the perfect time for children to learn the importance of being gentle, compassionate, and kind to the older dog, a lesson that will impact their response, later in life, to aging grandparents and parents.

Bringing Home a New Puppy

Many people prepare for the inevitable loss of an older pet by considering a new puppy, and I'm often asked whether this is a good idea. Personally, I think it's a good one, provided it's done before your dog is in a serious state of decline. Bringing the new dog in will help you perform a "changing of the guard," as your older dog's life draws to a close. But there are benefits for the older dog as well. A new puppy often gives the senior dog a new lease on life, making him perky and more interested in what's going on around him. He also may become more competitive, more affectionate, and more "puppyish" (in the good sense of that word). I think you'll find it does that for you as well, and rather than staying concentrated on your impending loss, you'll spend an equal amount of time delighting in the new addition to your pack. And, of course, when the time comes to grieve, your new pup will be there to see you through, with the unconditional love dogs always give so freely.

Until that happens, your older dog can serve as your assistant in training the new puppy. He knows the house rules already and he'll be quick to point them out to any new pup on the premises. I find there's often a spiritual link between an older dog and a new puppy in the family, with the pup taking on the traits of his senior sibling, taking cues from his behavior, following his lead, knowing when to be obedient and when to be playful. After all, he's got a great teacher in the dog that's lived with you for so many years.

When It's Time to Say Good-bye

The loss is inevitable, nevertheless impossibly difficult to face. There's something about losing a beloved pet that equates with no other experience. Among all our relationships, those with our pets are the only relationships in which we experience universal and unconditional acceptance. Your dog has never told you your faults, argued with you about your habits, or complained about your treatment of him. He's spent his whole life loving you. Not only that, he's been there at your side, every minute of every day that you were available to him. Not even the most loving family member can accomplish that feat. And now he's leaving you. But letting go is so terribly, terribly hard.

If you're lucky, he'll slip away quickly and gracefully. I believe dogs tell us when they're ready to move on. I also believe that they're waiting for our permission to go. But there are times when you're faced with a terrible decision: Is it time to put him down? Compassion will provide the answer. This is your beloved pet. You don't want him to suffer, and if he is in excruciating pain and the prognosis is hopeless, then there is no doubt that euthanasia is the only humane solution. Your veterinarian is the person who will tell you when it's time to take that final, terrible step and will help you through the grief. He's lost a good friend as well.

Coping with the Grief

Don't let anyone say to you, "Snap out of it! It's only a dog!" Nothing infuriates me more than hearing such an inane comment—a comment that only could be made by someone who hasn't had a close DogSpeak relationship. You've just lost your best friend. Trying *not* to feel the pain is illogical, unhealthy, and impossible. Personally, I believe in grieving for as long as it takes. When you've come to terms with your loss, the grieving will lessen, in its own due time. However, there are professionals who can help—social workers, psychologists, and groups linked to veterinary groups, medical centers, or even humane groups—who can talk you through the pain. There is absolutely no reason not to take the help that is available. When you've lost unconditional love, you've lost a great deal. On the other hand, having known unconditional love, you're certain to find it again. Be patient. Time is the great healer. And if you haven't gotten that new puppy already, you will, in your own right time. And the circle of life, and love, begins again.

Chapter 10

Simple Solutions to Common Problems

There are some problems so universal that they make up the majority of my training cases. Among these are aggression, destructive behaviors such as chewing and barking, pulling, jumping, and a common problem that lies at the root of many others: separation anxiety. Many of these "problem behaviors" are simply the dog's response to his genetics, those Eight Central Factors of Pack Behavior that control his instincts. You can take the dog out of the pack, but you really can't take the pack behavior out of the dog, and to the end of its days your dog will display behaviors that were useful to its wild ancestors, the wolves, but are frowned upon in our highly socialized culture. However, it helps to know that your dog isn't necessarily willful, disobedient, or just plain bad—he's a dog!

Just take a look at aggression, one of the most common, most serious, and most dangerous problems of all. Aggression in the wild keeps wolves alive. It also maintains order and structure within the pack, and the Alpha doesn't hesitate to use it to bring an intractable pack member in line. Aggression is a pure and primal instinct. It's also entirely unacceptable in your pet!

Now that you've learned DogSpeak, your understanding of the Eight Central Factors of Pack Behavior can make resolving behavior problems simple. You know that, as the Alpha leader, you must take control of your dog's hard-wired instincts and transform them into socially acceptable behaviors. With your new expertise in obedience training and your greater control of your dog, you now can use those skills to make your dog respond to your commands in a situation where his DNA tells him to do otherwise.

These are the most common dog behavior problems, and my simple solutions for resolving them.

Aggression

Aggression comes under many guises and takes many forms, such as dominance aggression, fear aggression, food-guarding aggression, and territorial aggression. Each behavior has a different cause, and each has a different, simple solution. Let's begin with dominance aggression, one of the most common and most dangerous of aggressive problems.

The Problem: Dominance Aggression

Alex came to me for help with his Border Collie mix, Sandy, who always tried to fight any dog he met in the street. It didn't seem to matter whether the other dog was male or female, large or small, the minute Sandy spotted another dog approaching, he lifted himself to full height, stuck his tail in the air, put his ears at "alert" and stiffened for the attack. The aggressive stance was followed by growling and lunging at the other animal, and Alex was convinced it was just a matter of time before a major fight ensued.

The DogSpeak Perspective

Here was a clear-cut case of dominance aggression. Sandy saw himself as top dog on the block, Alpha on his own turf, and he took great pains to establish his position immediately with any other dog in view. In addition, as Alpha dog, he viewed himself as his owner's protector, and his Alpha wolf instincts told him that if he wanted to maintain his status, he would have to fight for it on a daily basis. What Sandy didn't realize was that he wasn't a wolf and this wasn't the wild. Nor had he learned that his owner was the *real* Alpha-in-charge.

The Simple Solution

What Sandy really needed was a readjustment of his Alpha perspective and quick control and correction of his aggressive tendencies. That would involve more assertive behavior on the part of his owner in the form of stricter control. But in Sandy's case, there was an additional step to take. He'd never been neutered and my suggestion was to do so at once. It's a simple process which lowers hormonal output and lessens aggressive tendencies. (And no, it won't make your male dog a wimp!) In Sandy's case, that didn't resolve the problem. This top dog intended to remain just that! His owner and I moved to the next step: getting Sandy completely focused on Alex and making him understand that his owner was the *only* Alpha in their pack. We needed to teach Sandy to be entirely obedient to Alex and to respect all of his commands.

To gain maximum control of Sandy's Alpha-aggressive tendencies, I showed Alex how to high-collar him by placing the collar just under his chin and behind his ears. As we went through the basic obedience training, I showed Alex how to correct Sandy the instant he lunged for another dog. With

Sandy heeling at his left side, they set off on a walk. In no time at all, Sandy spotted another dog trotting down his side of the street. The DogSpeak warning signals went up: Sandy drew up to his most impressive height, ears snapped to alert, tail bushy and full, telegraphing to the stranger, "Keep away or fight." As he approached the other dog, he gave a low growl and lunged. At that exact moment, Alex snapped and jerked his leash and shouted "No!" It was the equivalent of an Alpha wolf's disciplinary snap at a subordinate who's made an aggressive move without pack permission or direction. Sandy was so startled, he stopped in his tracks, as Alex continued to keep him under tight, high-collared control. Alex had translated Alpha-wolf action into human language and had used behavior-shaping to correct Sandy's unacceptable behavior *while it was happening.* The immediacy of the correction is crucial since it gives the dog the message that his behavior will not be tolerated by his Alpha and that he must correct it immediately. As I had instructed him, Alex then gave Sandy the command to "Sit," using the DogSpeak gestures that are the essential part of the DogSpeak vocabulary. I was pleased to see that Sandy sat and looked up at Alex in an obedient, responsive, and respectful manner, entirely focused on his Alpha's next command. Alex praised his dog for his responsiveness and obedience, and gave me the high-sign as well. He'd just passed the first stage in resolving Sandy's aggression. Needless to say, it's the *repetition* of this immediate correction that, ultimately, will take the active aggression out of the dog. In some dogs, the aggressive instinct will always be present and must be tightly controlled for the dog's entire lifetime. Such was the case with Sandy and Alex, who had to fight to maintain his Alpha status by keeping Sandy under constant control. And Sandy never gave up the chance to threaten a fight—but he never got into one either.

If your dog views himself as Alpha, it's time to tighten your control and high-collar your dog until he learns *you* are the

Alpha leader of your pack. And if your obedience-training skills have dulled, by all means go back to "Basic Training Begins" (page 148) and sharpen them. Remember: The Alpha must maintain his control on a daily basis. And you're the Alpha!

The Problem: Fear Aggression

A new client, Carrie, called me in great distress. Her well-mannered little Bichon, Daisy, had tried to bite her. She'd never had one of her own dogs become aggressive and she couldn't understand this uncharacteristic, and clearly dangerous, behavior from a dog she'd now had for six months. As Carrie described the events that preceded the biting, I learned that she'd tried to spank Daisy for turning over the garbage. Daisy had crawled under a chair and when Carrie reached under to pull her out, she snapped. Carrie was too furious to be intimidated. She dragged the little dog out, gave her a smack on the rump, and locked her in the bathroom until she could find a trainer to offer advice. She found me.

Once I'd heard the story, I asked her to describe the dog's expression. Were Daisy's ears set forward or laid back against her skull? Was her muzzle drawn back and showing her teeth or open and snapping? When I heard her answers—the ears were laid back, the muzzle pulled back to show the teeth—I understood Daisy's problem.

The DogSpeak Perspective

My diagnosis: fear aggression. Daisy had been cornered under the chair. This big person was coming after her with arms raised. Daisy feared for her very life and thought she had no choice but to save herself by using her only available weapon, her teeth. In reality, Daisy was a very affectionate, entirely nonaggressive dog. But *any* dog which feels threatened will try to protect itself. Wouldn't you? That's why fear aggression is often found in street dogs, which are accustomed to being yelled at, kicked, bombarded with firecrackers, chased, and generally abused by people who don't want them around. Naturally, they too become self-protective. In all instances, what's lacking is trust.

The Simple Solution

In Daisy's case, the solution was to establish a strong, trusting relationship between her and her relatively new owner. We accomplished that by obedience training. At first, Carrie resisted. Why should she begin training when her dog, with this one unusual exception, was perfectly obedient? I explained that training creates trust. It allows the Alpha/owner to establish behavior parameters in a clear and loving way, establishing a strong bond between owner and canine companion that will last for a lifetime. Within a few sessions, Daisy and Carrie were working together as a perfectly paired unit. As follow-up, I prescribed three fifteen-minute obedience-training sessions a day to keep Daisy on her toes. I also pointed out that hitting a dog is never acceptable, but instructed Carrie that each time Daisy misbehaved, she was to have an immediate tune-up training session. This would work off her own anger and aggression while reinforcing to Daisy that she, Carrie, was Alpha of their pack. Within a month, Daisy was a different dog. Carrie reported to me with great excitement that Daisy seemed far more secure. Even more important, her garbage-trashing habit, which had been an attention-getting device, ceased. Daisy now got all the attention and praise she needed from her own positive behavior, and her trust in Carrie was established. This pack of two could move on to enjoy their lives together. Most important, Carrie learned, as I hope you will, that hitting a dog is *never* acceptable punishment. An intense obedience session is the proper productive solution and the best possible way to work off your annoyance with your pet.

The Problem: Territorial Aggression

Jenny loved the fact that her Wheaten Terrier, Murphy, wouldn't let strangers near the house. After all, Jenny lived alone in a somewhat isolated area and having a protective dog like Murphy made her feel safe. But when Murphy refused to let even the mailman approach the house, snarling furiously, biting at the fence, and generally displaying all the symptoms of rage, it was clear that Murphy had a problem that needed an immediate solution.

The DogSpeak Perspective

This was a clear case of territorial aggression and a very good example of pack behavior in action. Territorial behavior is one of the strongest of all behaviors, originating with wolves' need to protect their den and their young. It's an instinct that remains particularly strong in certain breeds such as terriers and other dogs bred as guard or herd dogs. It's also an instinct that is particularly pronounced in unaltered males. Murphy, with his terrier's instinct, envisioned himself as Jenny's pack-protector, which was good, but he'd taken it one level too far.

We needed to show Murphy the difference between sounding the alarm, which Jenny wanted, and out-and-out aggression, which was dangerous.

The Simple Solution

In Murphy's case, there were two solutions: neutering and obedience training. When I discovered Murphy had never been neutered, I recommended that as a first step, to cut down the hormonal output and reduce the natural aggression. Then Jenny and I undertook a series of obedience-training sessions to promote proper control on her part, as pack leader, and unquestioned obedience to her commands from Murphy. The most important step in controlling a territorial and aggressive dog is teaching the "Down/Stay," a command that serves as a successful control mechanism to prevent buildup of high-level aggression. I made sure that Jenny did this exercise on-leash at first, to assure control. Then I instructed her that when guests arrived, she should put Murphy in the Down/Stay position to show him she didn't need his protection at that moment. After several obedience lessons, Jenny was able to do that easily. Once Murphy had relaxed in the presence of the guests, Jenny instructed him to come to her side and "Sit," keeping him firmly by her side while the guests greeted him. Soon, Jenny was able to forgo the leash and simply put Murphy in a Down/Stay, where he remained quietly until she told him to "Sit." Murphy soon learned to be a sociable host, not a snarling guard dog, and the two developed an even closer relationship. Meanwhile Jenny's circle of friends were delighted and no longer afraid to visit. If your dog tends to be overprotective, this is a routine you can use to assure there'll be no unexpected aggression. Remember: A dog in Down/Stay is an obedient dog.

The Problem: Food-Guarding Aggression

The Andersen family was delighted with Katie, the adorable Springer Spaniel they'd adopted from the shelter. They couldn't believe their good luck and they also couldn't understand how she'd ended up in the shelter. Katie was affectionate, intelligent, responsive, and calm, with no indication at all that, lurking under her loving exterior, there was a very dark side. It surfaced one evening when Mrs. Andersen set Katie's food down on the kitchen floor and left. When she walked back into the kitchen a few minutes later, to her shock, Katie had turned into Cujo, snarling, snapping, and holding Mrs. Andersen at bay outside the kitchen. The Andersens were horrified and, frankly, frightened. They were on the phone to me within minutes.

The DogSpeak Perspective

My diagnosis: food-guarding aggression. Katie had reverted to her wolf ancestry and was guarding her food supply with every ounce of strength she had, as if this meal were her last. What the Andersens didn't know was that in her former home, Katie *did* have to fight for her food. She'd grown up in a household with ten other Springers and, being the runt of the litter, she often went hungry—until she learned to fight for her fair share. Her food-guarding instinct had developed far past what was necessary to keep her well-fed and happy and Katie became a textbook case of food-guarding aggression. In fact, as the Andersens later discovered, that was exactly why her former owners had dumped her at the shelter.

The Simple Solution

It's always wise to stop food-guarding aggression in pups before it gets a foothold. I do that by feeding a puppy directly from my hand, accustoming it to my being a part of the feeding process. With older dogs, it once again becomes a matter of creating an atmosphere of trust. You must teach the dog to trust you completely, so that he's willing to let you touch his bowl, or even remove the food, while he's eating.

To accomplish that, I gave Mrs. Andersen a new set of instructions for feeding Katie. She was to put on Katie's control collar and a six-foot leash before feeding her, then, holding the leash firmly, allow Katie to go to her food. I would keep my eye on the proceedings from outside the kitchen. As Katie started to eat, I asked Mrs. Andersen to approach her bowl. Immediately a low, warning rumble came from Katie's throat. As I'd instructed her, Mrs. Andersen gave a loud "No!" while simultaneously snapping the leash. This so startled Katie that she moved away from her bowl, which Mrs. Andersen quickly removed. After a minute, she replaced it and allowed Katie to continue eating. Each time she heard a growl, she repeated the lesson. After a couple of days, Katie realized that Mrs. Andersen was totally in charge and that she was entirely dependent on her owner for food. She also learned that as long as she didn't growl, Mrs. Andersen wouldn't take the food away from her. Soon Katie became reassured and much more calm. Once both the trust and Alpha status of Mrs. Andersen had been established, Katie became a loving, wonderful dog again, even at feeding time. The Andersens never experienced a repetition of the problem.

If you have a puppy, begin this exercise early in its life, so that your dog will know his food supply is always safe with you. But if, like the Andersens, you've acquired a grown dog with bad food-guarding habits, by all means repeat this exercise daily, over and over, until your dog allows you to stand near his food bowl while he's eating. After a while, you should be able to sit by him as he eats, move his bowl, or even remove it with no sign of aggression.

Kid-Safety Precaution

Unless you are absolutely certain your dog is trustworthy, *never* allow children to approach your dog's bowl while he's eating. It's better to be safe than very, very sorry.

Destructive Behavior

Destructive behavior takes many forms, from chewing the carpet (or the owner's best shoes) and clawing the stuffing out of the sofa to trashing the garbage or digging up the newly planted garden. It's all a result of a dog's natural exploratory instincts. But whether those instincts are allowed to become destructive depends on how well the dog was trained as a puppy.

Take chewing, for example. Chewing is normal dog behavior. It's an exploration of the environment, it feels good, and it relieves anxiety and tension. Puppies, particularly when they're teething, *need* to chew, and once they start, there's no telling where they stop. If that means going from the great-tasting upholstery straight through to the stuffing and then the wood itself, that, for a puppy, is fun. Just like babies, puppies learn about their environment through investigation, and in dogs (and babies), that investigation often involves chewing. Wolf pups in the wild chew sticks, they chew rocks and roots, and when they find a tasty bit of caribou bone, which provides calcium, they learn what it means to be a carnivorous wolf. Trouble is, when it's in your home and the tasty object is your sofa, *that's* not acceptable.

The Problem: Destructive Chewing

Jack was a successful stockbroker with a hectic schedule, one that had him dashing off to his office at 7:00 A.M., never returning before 7:00 P.M. So when he decided to get a puppy, his friends were skeptical. But Jack had fallen in love with an adorable Schnauzer pup and he was determined to make it a part of his busy life. He vowed to hire a canine caretaker who could walk the dog several times a day and feed it on schedule. Meanwhile, Jack had used my method of crating to housebreak his puppy, Helga, and it had been so successful that she was ready to graduate. Helga ould chill out in the den during the day and hang out in Jack's bedroom at night. Imagine Jack's shock when he returned home that first post-graduation evening to find the den virtually trashed. His expensive Oriental rug was in tatters, the leather sofa had been scratched until the stuffing spilled out, and litter from the trash basket—shredded by Helga—was scattered all over the floor. Worst of all, she'd discovered his favorite Gucci briefcase—the one he saved for special occasions—and gnawed off the corners. Jack was furious, with his first thought that this would be Helga's last day in *his* apartment. But when she looked up at him with her appealing big eyes, he couldn't bring himself to banish her. He called me instead.

The DogSpeak Perspective

I pointed out to Jack that puppies chew simply because that's what puppies do, an inheritance from their wolf ancestors. But in Helga's case, there was an additional element at work: She missed Jack! She was bored and she was inquisitive, a combination that was a problem waiting to happen. Where her crate environment had given her a safe haven for relaxing, now she had a big, beautiful place just inviting her to stick her nose into every corner and crevice. She couldn't wait to discover what this big new place was all about. Besides, the boundless energy that came with being seven months old wasn't spent by those ten-minute walks the caretaker gave her. Now she could work it off with some real puppy fun!

The Simple Solution

Jack needed to stop this destructive chewing immediately, otherwise his apartment would be history. I recommended that when Jack caught Helga in the act, he give a sharp "No!," which would surprise her and stop the action. Then he should redirect her with something designed for chewing, such as chew toys or bones. I also suggested he spray the furniture, and Helga's other favorite chew-spots, with one of the many dog-repellent sprays on the market. I knew the unpleasant taste would be a deterrent to her chewing proclivities.

The problem, basically, was Helga's boredom and her pent-up energy, which was venting itself destructively. As a remedy, I recommended that Jack take Helga for a long, energetic run each morning, pointing out that it would be a great health-booster for him as well. This would tire the puppy enough so that she'd sleep it off for the next few hours, until the dog walker arrived. Jack arranged that his caretaker walk Helga for at least thirty minutes, then return her to her crate until Jack returned in the evening, when he'd take her for another high-energy exercise session.

It was important for Helga and Jack to spend quality time together—after all, a lonely or bored puppy can get into plenty of trouble—while Helga learned what she could and couldn't chew. Basically, Helga needed a tune-up on her original training.

After a few days, I asked Jack to reverse the schedule: take Helga out for a short walk and return her to her crate. Later the dog walker would take Helga for a long, brisk walk and return her to the den where, once again, she'd sleep it off until Jack's return. In essence, we'd shifted Helga's free time to include both morning and afternoon. Now she was ready to have the run of the apartment, expanding her environment from her crate-den to the real den and eventually the whole apartment.

Within a few weeks, the transformation was accomplished

No-Chewing Tip

Never give a puppy an old shoe as a toy. He can't distinguish between an old one and the expensive pair you paid a fortune for just last week.

and Helga has never chewed any forbidden thing again. Of course, Jack keeps her supplied with good things to sink her puppy teeth into. I told Jack about the bones and hooves that can be found at pet shops and suggested he stuff them with tasty bits of cheese. These kept Helga amused for hours and by the time she'd gnawed them to nothing, she was exhausted.

Chewable toys can accomplish the same result, though it's important to be sure they're substantial enough so that the dog can't shred or swallow them. It's always best to ask your veterinarian for specific recommendations—after all, we don't want emergency abdominal operations in your future! I like heavy-duty rubber, which is practically indestructible and will last for a dog's lifetime.

The Problem: Destructive Digging

When Janice called me, I could hear the anger and stress in her voice. "I've just gotten my new flower garden completed—it cost me a fortune!—and when I walked out this morning, I found that my Jack Russell, Skipper, had dug up practically all the plants. There were holes everywhere! What on earth got into him? I'm so mad I almost feel like getting rid of him." I could understand her feelings, all right. I also understood what had caused the problem.

The DogSpeak Perspective

The moment I heard "Jack Russell," I knew that digging was second nature to Skipper. He was a terrier, after all, and that's exactly where the word terrier comes from—*terra,* or soil. Most terriers were bred to dig and this is one instinct so hard-wired that every terrier owner must combat it from the start.

It's especially true when there's good, fresh, just-turned soil to dig in, and if the gardener has added manure to the mix, that's almost irresistible. The effect it had on Skipper was much like catnip to a kitten. I guessed that Skipper probably had done more than dig. Probably, just like his wolf ancestors, he'd bathed himself in this interesting new scent by rolling in the soil he'd dug. It was great fun for Skipper but great expense and even greater annoyance for his owner. If Skipper wanted to keep his good home, he needed to change his ways!

The Simple Solution

We had to teach Skipper that digging—at least, digging in the garden—is never acceptable. I suggested that Janice put Skipper on a leash and lead him around the garden, pointing to each freshly-dug hole and saying "No digging!" This tactic is not punishing him after the fact; it's warning him that, in future, such behavior will not be tolerated. I also suggested that Janice blow up a dozen or so balloons and bury them in shallow holes in Skipper's favorite digs, covering them lightly with soil or leaves. Sure enough, the next time Skipper sneaked into the garden to do his dirty digging, the balloons exploded. It was sufficient to give him the message: "No digging here!"

An Alternative Anti-Digging Device

An alternative, but equally simple, solution for destructive digging is to place ordinary mothballs under the plants. The scent is so strong that it will deter not only terriers but numerous other destructive varmints that wander into your garden when no one's looking.

A couple of weeks later, Janice phoned me to say that Skipper had had quite enough of his "explosive" behavior and had gone on to other, less destructive, entertainments.

The Problem: Excessive Barking . . .

Fluffy drove her owners, the Browns, absolutely wild. She barked constantly—when anyone passed in the hallway, when the doorbell rang, when visitors arrived, when she spotted another dog in the street, when the mailman dropped off the mail, when her owners came home, or even when they went out. Fluffy just barked most of the time, and it was getting on everyone's nerves. Her owners were considering finding a country home for Fluffy, but first they asked whether I could help.

The DogSpeak Perspective

My diagnosis: Fluffy never had been taught that "No" means *"No!,"* as in "no barking." She saw barking as a terrific way to get her owners' attention and she had taken the natural vocalization instincts of her wolf ancestors to a limit that was both unnecessary and unacceptable. In barking to alert her owners to approaching strangers, Fluffy was using her territorial pack behavior, and using it correctly. But she needed to be shown when to bark, and when to stop.

The Simple Solution

The first step: Teach Fluffy to respect the word "No." From now on, when she barked appropriately, she would be praised by the Browns. When she didn't, she'd get a strict lesson in obedience. For example, when Fluffy heard footsteps in the hallway outside the apartment, her territorial instincts told her to alert the Browns. I suggested that one of them always go to the door, look outside, then praise Fluffy for her alert bark. The trouble was, Fluffy often didn't stop with the alert, but became more hysterical and out of control the longer her barking continued. To remedy that, we needed to set the stage with a situation the Browns could control and from which Fluffy would learn the difference between acceptable and unacceptable barking. Up until now, there had been no restraints on Fluffy. We were about to change that.

First, I had Fluffy's owners put her on leash. Then I asked Mrs. Brown to leave the apartment and go down to the lobby, while Mr. Brown and I stayed with Fluffy. On cue, the bell rang and Fluffy began her shrieking barks. At that moment, and at my direction, Mr. Brown clapped his hands loudly near Fluffy's head, then immediately jerked the leash and shouted, "No!" Fluffy was so startled, she stopped barking. The moment she did, Mr. Brown put her into a Sit position, told her to stay, and then praised her for her impeccable behavior. It was the beginning of a new life for Fluffy. After a few more such lessons, Fluffy had gotten the no-barking message, and Mr. Brown was delighted that his course in obedience training, particularly the "Sit/Stay" command, had served a real and useful purpose. Of course, whenever Fluffy alerted to a real problem, she received abundant praise. And since she no longer was a problem herself, the bond between Fluffy and her owners deepened and grew stronger. Now theirs really is a happy home!

. . . And Howling

Other problem barking, or even howling, may be the result of an entirely different dynamic. For example, Stephen called me in despair because his landlord had threatened to evict him. Seems that Otto, his Weimaraner, began barking the moment Stephen left for work each morning, and never let up until his master returned home. It didn't matter that a dog-walker came around for the midday walk. Otto missed Stephen and showed it by barking or, from time to time, letting out the most pitiful howls. Now they were going to lose their apartment, and Stephen was desperate.

The DogSpeak Perspective

Here was a clear case of separation anxiety, one of the most common causes of problem barking or howling. As always, it has its roots in wolf-pack behavior. In the wild, wolves use a howl, or a yipping bark, to say, "Here I am. Come on back to the den" or "Where are you? Help me find you" or even "I'm alone here. Let's get the pack together." Basically, a howling dog is saying the same thing.

The Simple Solution

The basic ingredient in curing separation anxiety is teaching the dog to understand that he is secure and you *will* come back home to him. Building confidence is requisite, and, surprisingly, the best way to do that is through obedience training. Just as a child feels insecure when his parents don't seem to be in charge, so a dog prefers an Alpha leader who sets the rules and is capable of enforcing them—a *strong* Alpha leader, who demonstrates he can take good care of him.

The first thing Stephen needed to do was teach Otto to accept his absence. The best tool for that is the crate, which becomes a safe and secure den. I asked Stephen to crate Otto each morning when he left for work. The caretaker would take Otto out to feed, water, and walk him, always returning the dog to his crate for the afternoon. Stephen rebelled at first, reluctant to keep the energetic Otto confined. But I persuaded Stephen to give it a short trial. What astonished Stephen was that Otto didn't sit in his crate and howl. However, I had taken the precaution of instructing Stephen on what to do if he did. At the first howl, Stephen should return to the crate, open the door, put his hand firmly around Otto's muzzle, just the way an Alpha wolf would do, and give a firm command, "No!" As it happened, Otto simply settled in with his blanket and chew toys and seemed perfectly comfortable, secure that in his den he was safe.

Eventually, Stephen was able to transfer the crate/den experience to a room—in this case, the kitchen—and later to include the whole apartment. After a couple of weeks, the problem was solved and Stephen and Otto were both secure and happy. No more complaining landlords!

The Problem: Jumping

Lucy, a Tibetan Terrier, jumped up on everything and everybody. She had become the nuisance of the neighborhood and no amount of well-intentioned (though ineffective) correction by her owner seemed to stop her—at least, not in time. Lucy had left mud on strangers' clothes, paw prints on her owner Sandra's best suede skirt, and runs in all her friends' pantyhose. But Lucy also jumped up on kids and—it had been just a matter of time—finally had knocked over a small child. The child was terrified, his mother enraged. Lucy was becoming a menace and the time had come to take serious action. Fortunately, Sandra had me in her Rolodex.

The DogSpeak Perspective

Lucy was a gregarious and energetic dog. She loved people, loved life, and loved to show it, which she did by jumping up to express her joy, just the way her wolf relatives do when they greet one another. Wolves sniff each other, touch each other, lick each other to express their affection. But in a dog/human relationship, that doesn't quite work. Since humans are in another height realm, Lucy needed to jump up to reach that human muzzle-equivalent, the face, so she bounced up and down like a jumping jack to reach the object of her affection (and there were many such objects!). Lucy simply didn't know that expressing her feelings in this manner is not proper canine behavior. People were glad to see Lucy, and liked her enthusiastic acceptance, but they were *not* happy with the mud-covered result. But since it's hard to resist such an exuberant greeting and so much unconditional love, many of her targets found Lucy's behavior adorable, a fact that reinforced Lucy's belief that jumping is A-OK behavior. It was time to call a halt.

The Simple Solution

The first step in solving the problem: Teach Lucy not to jump on Sandra. Later, we'd expand that to include other people. The difficulty was in showing Lucy she must not jump, while still letting her know that her greeting was most welcome.

I asked Sandra to greet Lucy by kneeling to her level. This gave Lucy the opportunity to offer an ebullient "welcome home" to her owner *without* the jumping. I pointed out that we could ask other friends to use the same technique for a while, until Lucy learned that jumping wasn't a necessary ingredient in a reciprocated greeting.

But obviously not everyone wanted to kneel to Lucy. We needed to correct the jumping permanently. For that, I asked Lucy's owner to do the following: When she opened the door and Lucy began her "run to jump," she was to extend both arms stiffly, out and downward towards Lucy, while simultaneously giving the sharp command "No jumping!," followed by the "Sit" and "Stay" commands. Then she was to go down to Lucy's level to receive her effusive "welcome home." (Owners who either can't or don't want to get down to dog level may simply lean down toward the dog.)

This worked for Lucy. But in the case of Jason, a huge Shepherd, it didn't do the trick. To his owner, Mitch, I suggested that the moment Jason jumped up, he grab the dog's front paws and hold them, firmly saying "No jumping!" Then he was to make Jason sit and stay. When he obeyed, Mitch was instructed to praise him by saying "What a good dog!" In no time, Jason also was transformed and his neighborhood was far more serene and safe. No matter how innocent a dog's motives, jumping can be dangerous, especially when a big dog jumps on a small child or a fragile, elderly person. Jumping just isn't socially acceptable canine behavior, no matter what that wolf instinct says.

Jealousy

Jealousy is a big, bad word, for people *and* dogs. And while jealousy is jealousy, invariably caused by insecurity (again, in people and dogs), with dogs it takes many destructive forms. There are separate solutions for each.

The Problem: Jealousy of Another Adult

Lorraine sounded frantic. She'd finally found the man of her dreams and they'd decided to get married, but her Bull Mastiff, Rochester, had taken a strong dislike to her fiance, Peter, and the more Peter made himself at home at Lorraine's house, the more aggressive Rochester became. The final straw was when Peter leaned over to kiss Lorraine and Rochester jumped up, positioned himself between the two, and gave a low, guttural growl. Peter and Lorraine were both stopped cold, afraid to make a move. Here was a serious situation indeed, and a dangerous one as well. It couldn't be allowed to escalate.

The DogSpeak Perspective

This was a clear illustration of jealousy in action. Up until recently, Rochester and Lorraine had been the only members of their pack. Yes, her friends visited, but they also went away again, and there was never any question of their replacing Rochester in Lorraine's affections. Now here was another human who, seemingly, had moved in to stay. Rochester saw it as a clear threat to his pack position as top dog.

The Simple Solution

In order to re-establish pack order, Peter and Rochester needed to establish their own bond. I asked that Peter take Rochester for long, companionable walks. Peter also needed to establish himself as co-owner with Lorraine by feeding Rochester, brushing him, and caring for him. But, most important of all, Peter needed to develop the same skills in handling Rochester that

Lorraine had. For that, Peter needed in-tandem obedience training to familiarize himself with the signals to which Rochester had learned to respond. By doing this, we began to create a new structure for their pack, making Peter co-Alpha with Lorraine and establishing Rochester's trust in this new pack order. Not only did Peter go through the same training exercises that Lorraine had years before, but he learned the importance of the "Go to Your Place" command. That kept Rochester from becoming involved in any affectionate gestures between Peter and Lorraine and gave everyone greater peace of mind.

The process was so successful that Peter insisted Rochester be a member of the wedding. And so it was that on their wedding day, the big dog sat at Peter's side, quiet, obedient, and loving. And yes, they all did live together happily ever after!

The Problem: Jealousy of a New Baby

Susan and Arnold had been proud parents for years, ever since they first adopted their beloved Chow-Shepherd mix, Tara. For five years, Tara had been the focus of their lives, and they took her everywhere with them, even on vacations. But now Susan was pregnant and she and Arnold were wondering how Tara would accept a new member of the family. If she didn't accept the baby, her size alone could make the situation explosive. A very worried Susan sought my help, and I was delighted that she called me three months before her due date.

The DogSpeak Perspective

Tara saw herself as the most important member of this three-member pack, and Susan and Arnold had done everything to reinforce that impression, doting on her, never going anywhere without her, giving her their undivided attention. Tara had her special bed, her toy box filled with chew toys, balls, and other goodies, and her every wish was her owners' command. Naturally, Tara, who'd never experienced having another "baby" in the house, wasn't likely to be pleased. She would see this as competition for her position as the Beta, or second-in-command, in this pack.

Meanwhile, Susan's hormones were busy establishing her as a new mother and Tara, with a dog's supersensitivity, picked up on these changes, becoming even more attached to her human mom and even more protective. This was a difficult situation in the making and its outcome would depend on our teaching Tara to accept, embrace, and protect this future new member of the pack.

The Simple Solution

First, it was important to teach Tara control and restraint. She'd had no obedience training and that was where we began. Once Tara had learned basic control, we focused on the commands "Down/Stay" and "Go to Your Place and Down/Stay." These were the commands that would help Susan and Arnold keep Tara safely under control while they attended to the baby's needs. Later, these commands would allow Tara to lie quietly at Susan's feet as she was feeding the baby, creating additional bonding between Tara and the baby and making Tara protective of this new, helpless creature.

Meanwhile, I instructed Susan how to prepare Tara for the baby's homecoming. Susan was to place Tara on a leash and, tightly controlling the dog, introduce her to the baby. It was important that Tara sniff the baby and absorb the baby's unique infant scent. In the wild, wolf mothers allow other pack members to sniff and greet new pups, a ritual that creates pack acceptance of the new addition. Pack protocol demanded that Tara receive the same sort of ritualized introduction to her newest pack-member sibling.

I also asked Susan to let Tara sniff the baby's soiled diapers. This would be the human equivalent of a wolf's sniffing the pups' feces and urine, which confirms that this indeed is a delicate, helpless new member of the pack and that other pack members must be cautious and protective of it. Once Tara had accepted her responsibilities to the baby, I had no doubt that she would serve as a wonderful "nanny," always ready to alert Susan to the baby's needs. It was equally important that Tara be included in every aspect of the baby's care so that she would never feel excluded, never fear for her position in the pack nor resent her new sibling.

Susan and Arnold phoned me when the baby was a few weeks old to say that the process had been an amazing success and that the new four-member pack was a very happy family indeed.

The Problem: Pulling On-Leash

Fern called me sobbing. Her newly adopted dog, Annie, had turned out to be a newly acquired pain. Fern had lost her beloved poodle just a month before and had been devastated, so I was very pleased indeed when she informed me she'd fallen in love again, with an adorable terrier mix she found at the shelter. Of course, the minute I met her new dog, I knew Fern had taken on a handful. One look at Annie's eyes told me this new dog was a would-be Alpha who would resist Fern at every turn. She was a far cry from the perfectly behaved lady that Fern's former dog had been. "I just can't cope, Bash," Fern was saying. "She's attacking every other dog on the street and she's pulled so hard that my back has gone out and every walk is an agony. What am I going to do?" What I fervently wished she had done was consult me *before* the adoption. But now we had to work to socialize Annie, and quickly, before Fern gave up on the relationship.

The DogSpeak Perspective

Annie was born a dominant dog, a characteristic common with terriers, which are bred to be feisty, independent, and tough. Given the slightest opportunity, terriers *always* try to control any situation. In this case, it was crucial that we reverse the roles, making Annie see Fern as her undisputed Alpha. Fern had to take control of Annie, not the other way around. As a first step, I needed for Fern to understand that Annie was *not* her beloved poodle, and that where her first dog had been a cooperative pack follower, Annie was determined to be the leader of their pack of two. I needed to teach Fern the skills and techniques that would let her be an assertive Alpha leader—one who could make Annie accept her commands. Annie's pulling had to stop and Fern had to take control.

The Simple Solution

We had to keep in mind Annie's background. She'd been returned to the shelter once, so there was no history on her. For all we knew, she'd been living on the streets, forced to defend herself against other, bigger dogs. That could be contributing to her need to pull aggressively towards all other dogs on the street. (It's the old "If I get them first, they can't get me" theory at work.)

We began with basic obedience training, teaching Annie to walk calmly at Fern's side. For maximum control, I showed Fern how to high-collar Annie. Then, beginning with the simple commands of "Heel," "Sit," and "Stay," we taught Annie the basics of obedience, later proceeding to more complex exercises. In one such exercise, Annie was asked to walk in and out of obstacles. Such an exercise would increase Fern's control of Annie and teach Annie to walk through crowds and past other dogs calmly and without breaking her stride. To combat her aggressive tendencies, we added group classes to her regular training sessions. These would be key in socializing Annie. In this highly structured group situation, Annie discovered that, no matter how much she was tempted to lunge at other dogs, she and all other members of the group were tightly controlled. Since this group situation replicated a pack, Annie's inherited follow-the-pack-leader instincts responded positively. At the same time, Fern's role as Annie's Alpha leader was established within the group/pack.

Fern was astonished by Annie's immediate change of attitude. The little terrier marched proudly around the group circle, winding through the in-and-out exercise which brought her in close proximity to other, much larger dogs. She seemed to understand that, in this situation and with Fern showing greater control, she was safe. It was the beginning of Annie's complete transformation.

Fern called me a year later to say that she and Annie had just celebrated their first anniversary. "I never thought I could love her this much," she said, "but I'm kind of worried. She's so mellow . . . do you think she's okay?" I couldn't help laughing!

Pulling is a bad habit that must be brought in line. The best solution for it is high-collaring, plus a steady basic obedience routine. It's the clearest way of showing your dog just who really is in charge!

The Problem: Separation Anxiety

Separation anxiety is a common problem that often is at the root of many other problems, such as destructive chewing. Many dogs find it difficult to comprehend that the owner who leaves really *will* return, and their fears and insecurities are expressed in destructive ways. Separation anxiety was at the core of Daisy's destructive garbage-trashing, Otto's hysterical barking, and Helga's destructive chewing.

The DogSpeak Perspective

Separation anxiety is a direct product of a dog's DNA. His ancestors, the wolves, are social (and sociable) animals. Isolate a "lone wolf" and you will have an unhappy one who often responds to his situation with piteous howls in the night. Your dog's genetics have hard-wired him to be in the company of a pack, whether canine or human, and when he's isolated from it (or you), he panics. He may feel abandoned, becoming nervous and anxious, responding as his genes have taught him, by howling or barking. Or he may find relief from his anxiety by nonstop chewing or other destructive behaviors. If his anxiety is truly severe, he may urinate, vomit, or develop diarrhea. He isn't being bad. He simply can't help himself. He's very, very scared.

So Serena discovered when she took her little Maltese, Phoebe, for a weekend trip to a friend's house. All was well until Serena and her friend went out to dinner. When they returned, Phoebe was cowering under the bed. She'd turned over the trash basket, shredded every piece of paper in the house, and urinated on the rugs. Serena was in shock. Phoebe had always been such a well-behaved little dog, a perfect lady in all situations. And she'd never ever messed in the house. Serena was embarrassed, upset, and angry. But through her anger, she could see Phoebe's fear. When she got back to town, she called me at once.

The Simple Solution

As I told Serena, resolving separation anxiety calls for compassionate reassurance. Though Phoebe was quite accustomed to being alone in her own house (which she felt was her safe-and-secure den), she'd never experienced being left in a strange place. I wasn't surprised that she had panicked.

In this case, my solution was for Serena to travel with Phoebe's crate. It was a familiar place in which she automatically would feel at home. Dogs don't like change, and anything that takes them out of their environment and away from their owner, or interrupts their accustomed schedule, can throw them into a frenzy. The usual result: bathroom accidents, destructive behaviors, and general chaos. The solution always is to provide a safe haven for your dog and to reassure him that you always will come back to him.

It's always best to condition a dog as a puppy to accept your absence, but the technique is the same for pups or older dogs. Begin in your own environment, leaving your dog for just fifteen minutes at a time. Gradually extend those absences to longer periods. You must be sure that you've taken care of your dog's physical needs *before* you leave. Feed him, water him, take him for a long walk to get his exercise and relieve himself.

After all, a dog that's desperate to go to the bathroom will be far more anxious than one that's comfortable. (Surely you've experienced such moments!) When you finally go, leave him his favorite chew toys (there are great chew toys that can be filled with cheese or liver treats to keep a dog amused for hours). Pretty soon your dog will learn to trust that you won't leave him in the lurch—without food, desperate for the bathroom, or lonely and bored. Instead, you're leaving him comfortable, settled in to chew on his goodies, and probably thinking, "Say, this isn't so bad. Every time she goes away, I get all this good stuff."

But if you're leaving your dog in a strange place, where he has no reason to feel safe and secure, a crate is the best possible solution. If a crate isn't available, or it isn't practical to travel with one, then you might consider confining him in a space within the house (or hotel or motel) you're visiting. The same rules still apply: Feed, water, and walk *before* you go, talk to him soothingly, provide him with plenty of toys for entertainment, and give him a snug, safe den to nestle into.

Above all else, be sure that your dog gets obedience training. It remains the perfect tool for teaching your dog that when he's in your care, he's perfectly safe. Teaching him to "Sit/Stay" or "Go to Your Place" while you go about your daily routine at home will show him clearly that separation isn't forever. And it isn't so bad after all.

Mischief, Mischief!

Some dogs just can't help themselves. They always get into mischief! They aren't bad dogs, only curious, lively, and inquisitive creatures who get into habits that drive their owners wild—climbing up on kitchen counters, stealing food from the table or from the garbage, jumping up on the furniture, sleeping on the bed. They don't even know they're misbehaving; they're dogs and they'll take as much as we'll give them. It's up to us, the Alphas in their lives, to teach them the parameters. Trouble is, we often lay out those parameters with mixed messages.

The Problem: Stealing Food from the Table or Kitchen Counter

Let's say you're having a party and you've arranged the food beautifully on the table. Here comes McDuff, your sheepdog, nose twitching, bouncing with enthusiasm. It's a party! And he expects to take part, envisioning one bite for you and one for him. Naturally, the moment you turn your back, an entire plate of hors d'oeuvres disappears.

The DogSpeak Perspective

For McDuff, this is a wolf-pack gathering, sharing the fruits of the hunt at a group feast. It's natural that McDuff not want to be left out. In fact, he wants to get there first. That's how his genes tell him to respond.

The Simple Solution

Obviously, McDuff should have been taught, from the outset, that food on the table is *not* his. But there's still an opportunity to break McDuff of his food-stealing habits. It first requires teaching McDuff basic obedience and concentrating on the "Down/Stay" and "Go to Your Place" commands. With those lessons learned, you are in control of where McDuff is during the party. Practice by setting a tempting morsel of food on the table then telling McDuff to go to his place. This will keep his paws off, and nose out, of the party food and let your guests enjoy what they came for. But of course, at the end of the evening, it would be polite to reward McDuff with his own doggie treat, just for being a good, obedient dog. (Remember, though, don't give him food from the table—that's just an invitation to steal!)

The Problem: Trashing the Garbage

You come home after a very hard day at the office to find, waiting just inside the front door, a trail of odorous garbage. Your sweet little Beagle, Josie, is nowhere to be seen. It's the last straw! And if you could find her, you'd let her know it.

The DogSpeak Perspective

Josie was feeling the pull of the wolf pack. With wolves, anything fragrant is something to be investigated and Josie did exactly as her DNA ordered her to do. She checked it out. Never mind that checking it out meant dragging it *all* out and spreading it across the floor. Of course, once she'd accomplished her exciting adventure, Josie went under the chair—her favorite den—to sleep it off.

The Simple Solution

There's no point in correcting Josie now. The only effective time for correction is when a mischievous act is in progress. However, you can find ways to make garbage less attractive. Spray it with a repellant or sprinkle mothballs on top of it. This will diffuse the tempting odor of garbage and deter any further investigations. Or you can set a harmless trap designed to show Josie, in terms she'll understand, that the garbage is off-limits and not an area she should investigate. This one requires a set-up. Blow up a balloon and put it in the garbage. Then show Josie the garbage can and tell her that it's a "No! No!" Now open the lid and pop the balloon. Josie isn't going to like that a bit and will be more hesitant about approaching it next time. To be on the safe side, the next time you leave for the office, place a blown-up balloon in the garbage. The moment Josie puts her claws into it, "Bam!" It usually takes only a couple of tries before this mischief becomes not so much fun. But when Josie discovers that you now praise her when you come home, she won't mind at all.

The Problem: Jumping on the Bed or the Furniture

You've just had all your furniture reupholstered in a superexpensive fabric. The next thing you know, your Basset Hound, Albert, has made it look twenty years old. You know you have only yourself to blame, since from the time he was a puppy you've allowed Albert on the furniture. So how's he going to know the difference between the old, comfortable furniture he thought was his and this fancy new-looking stuff? He isn't.

Or let's say you absolutely refuse to let your dog sleep in your bed. Yet every time you leave the house, that's exactly where he goes. Trouble is, when you come home, he's sitting placidly by the door. The only way you know he's guilty is that your pillows are tossed about and there's a nice round indentation where he's been sleeping. It wouldn't take a private eye to figure that one out!

The DogSpeak Perspective

Dogs like to nest. Unless your dog has special bedding where he feels comfortable and secure, he'll find a special place—on your furniture or your bed. And since both retain your unmistakable scent, the feeling of having you close will be even more alluring.

The Simple Solution

The simplest solution is to give your dog a comfortable, cozy, cushioned place of his own and, if need be, use a crate to break him of his unacceptable habit of jumping on the furniture or the bed. Tell him to go to his place and, when he does, praise him lavishly. Later, you'll be able to bring the bedding out of the crate and keep it near you on the floor.

If you've just re-covered your dog's favorite sleeping spot, the sofa, help him adjust to its new off-limits status—a concept your dog can't comprehend—by making a pillow from the old fabriç for his exclusive use. Again, tell him to go to his place and show him clearly that his place is on the old sofa-cover, *not* the newly covered sofa. By the way, some dogs are happiest (and most secure) sleeping on their owners' clothing. It's reassuring. A worn-out sweatshirt makes a great doggie bedspread, but *don't* wash it first. It's your familiar scent they long for.

The most important thing of all is to establish your own parameters before you bring a dog into your life. Some of the most loving dog owners are repelled by the thought of sleeping with a dog. Others find they can't sleep without that warm body snuggled against them. Some are fastidious about their houses—that's no place for a dog, they think—while others give the dog the run of the house. Only you can decide what works best in your household. But once that's established, let your dog know right from the beginning where he is, and isn't, welcome to place his paws. If you cuddle your dog on the sofa one minute, then ban him from it when it's been re-covered, he's not only going to be confused, he's going to continue the behavior that has been acceptable for years. If you allowed him on the bed when he was a cute and cuddly puppy and then, just because he grew to 165 pounds, banned him from it, he isn't going to understand this sudden switch in signals. And he'll be a very confused dog indeed (while he'll still use every opportunity to take over the bed).

With dogs, clarity is the essential order of the day. Straight talk, clear commands, and absolutely no mixed signals! And at the basis of it all, one all-important tool: obedience training. If you take it seriously and practice it diligently, you and your dog will develop a loving bond of trust that will make your relationship as close to perfect as life gets.

Chapter 11

On to the Future

You and your dog have come a long way together since you had your first lesson in DogSpeak. The housebreaking is accomplished, the obedience lessons learned, the problems all resolved, the trust established. And suddenly you look down one day at the dog trotting along beside you and you realize, "We're in tune!" Isn't that a wonderful feeling? Yours is a DogSpeak relationship, a perfectly attuned partnership in which you live together, play together, work together, and love together as a perfectly synchronized team. And now your commitment to this relationship pays off, as you move forward into new worlds to explore, new delights to experience, and ever deeper love to feel. Now you can include your dog in almost everything you do, and take him almost everywhere you go, from your office to your vacation getaway.

Playtime

Dogs have a joyous response to life that we all would do well to emulate. Like wolves, who play to learn the skills of life, dogs at play are learning to interact, to communicate, to develop closer relationships, greater agility, alertness, quickness, and a happy attitude. Interestingly, research has shown that dogs left to play alone, or even with another dog, soon lose interest when their human companion isn't around. It's you they want as a playmate, and this play interaction not only creates trust, it relieves tension and stress (in both of you) and works off a dog's abundant energy.

Since dogs love to work almost as much as they love to play, a play experience that combines the two is ecstasy for a dog. Today there's an increasing number of interesting and challenging places for play, from doggie playgrounds with agility courses to dog parks and runs. I love to see dogs work on agility courses. When you see their delighted expressions as they work the maze, climb the seesaw, crawl through the tunnels, and leap triumphantly over the final jumps, you'll understand how important play—even hard-work play—is to your dog. I always advise my clients to devote some time each week to ritualized play, where dogs can be with other dogs and can put their considerable physical prowess to work at hard play. Call the American Kennel Club, check out the Internet, or call dog organizations and clubs in your community for agility courses or dog playgrounds in your area.

Dog runs are gathering places for the canine pack and they're best when enclosed and closely supervised. Here, dogs run free, making new acquaintances, renewing old friendships, running, chasing, wrestling, and sniffing, delighted just in being dogs. And while the dogs are catching up on the latest doggie headlines, the owners also are making new friends. (I'm sure you already know that a dog is one of the most effective matchmakers on earth.)

By now, it's routine to see people jogging, hiking, biking, or just strolling, all in the company of their canine companions. The dogs, of course, are delighted to be included, since they want to be wherever their Alpha/owner is. But occasionally owners forget to consider their dogs' limits. My heart goes out to the panting dog running along beside his owner's bike in 100-degree weather. This is supposed to be play, not punishment, so before you take your dog along for any strenuous activity, *always* consider the dog's limitations, especially in extreme weather.

On Vacation

It's routine these days for people to share vacations with their pets. In fact, there are even camps for owners and dogs, designed to provide quality vacation time for both, in one another's inimitable company. An increasing number of hotels and motels accept canine companions as honored guests and some even provide elegant doggie amenities, from special menus to four-poster beds and private white-gloved walkers (for which you pay handsomely!). However, traveling with your dog does require careful planning, and whether you're going by car or plane, please be sure to make your "dogs accepted" reservations well in advance, so that your dog will be assured of a warm welcome.

Before you even consider travel plans, be sure your dog's inoculations are up to date and his health checks out A-OK, and be absolutely certain he has proper identification that's clear and visible.

By Car

With DogSpeak, you've already taught your dog to be a first-class traveler—you did that when you gave him the crate that became his den/home. And since the safest way for a dog to travel, whether by car or plane, is in a crate, your dog will feel at home and secure no matter how far you roam. The crate will be both his home away from home and a safety precaution for him and for you, the driver. It will prevent any accidents that could result from sudden swerves and stops while it discourages your dog from climbing into the front seat with you—not a safe move when you're flying down the interstate!

If your dog isn't accustomed to riding in a car, then by all means introduce him to the experience with a series of short prevacation trips. Remember to lessen the chance of car sickness by keeping his food and water to a minimum before the ride. Even on short trips, stop occasionally for him to relieve himself. Once he's become a "roader," you can plan the long drive. If you have an SUV or a station wagon, do as dog-show professionals do and make the crate your dog's private travel compartment. However, if yours is a compact car and the crate just won't fit, it's imperative that you teach your dog to lie quietly on the back seat, on the special bedding you've brought along for the trip. That will require a few lessons using the "Down/Stay" command, first while the car's parked, then later while it's in motion. If he jumps around in the back, stop the car and repeat the "Down/Stay" command until he learns that travel is about obeying your commands, and if he wants to come along, he'll have to follow the rules. Of course, the simplest and surest solution is a seat belt or doggie car seat, both of which you can obtain through any pet-supply catalog.

On trips, as always, you must provide regular food and water, and you'll need to make regular bathroom stops as well. One important safety caution: Never leave your dog alone in the car, even for a short time. It isn't safe. You'd be surprised how many dogs are stolen from locked cars. And of course, *never* leave your dog in the car in hot weather, even for a single minute. With their 102-degree normal temperature, dogs overheat quickly and are far more susceptible to heat exhaustion and stroke than humans. If you're traveling alone with your dog, please take that into account and plan your trip accordingly. Since dogs never are allowed in restaurants, you'll be eating in transit. You can pack food for you both in insulated bags or, on the journey, have your hotel pack a lunch. Be sure to include enough bottled water for the two of you. Then, when you're both getting hungry, find a shady rest stop and have a relaxing picnic.

There are many organizations, such as AAA or humane groups, that will give you information on hotels and motels that accept pets. Travel agents and the Internet are both good resources. But be sure to plan in advance! Many places limit the number of canine guests.

By Plane

Dogs are becoming frequent flyers these days as more and more people are taking their pets along for the flight. With plane travel, there are regulations that must be followed and stipulations that must be met, and it's essential to check these out in advance before heading for the airport with your dog. All airlines charge a fee for carrying a dog in the cabin and, as a rule, only one dog is permitted on board for any given flight. Dogs must be in enclosed carriers and must be small enough to fit under the seat (20 pounds is the limit on most airlines). If your dog is a large one, he won't be going in the seat next to you unless he's a certified guide, hearing, or assistance dog. He can, however, fly in the baggage compartment. For that, dogs must travel in crates, and since your dog already views his crate as home, he won't be stressed by this new experience. Though many people are reluctant to ship their pets as baggage, the most coddled and costly show dogs travel this way. However, it's important to take certain precautions. Avoid flying your dog in extreme weather, hot *or* cold. If you're traveling during the summer-vacation months, book a flight that's either early morning or late evening, and always try to book nonstop flights, to avoid the additional stress of your dog's being transferred from one plane to another.

Before any plane trip, have your dog checked thoroughly by your veterinarian. You will need a certificate of all vaccinations and shots to date, which allows you to travel from one state to another. For international travel, check with the embassy of the country you plan to visit. Some countries, such as the United Kingdom, place stringent quarantines on animals. It's better to leave your pet at home in such a case.

Feeding your dog just before a flight is *not* recommended, since the stress of a new experience may cause vomiting and other stomach distress. Feed him several hours before you leave for the airport, then make sure he's had time to relieve himself before being loaded on board so that he'll be comfortable en route. Naturally, airport personnel will make sure your dog has water in his crate's water dish.

Off to Work

When you're in a DogSpeak relationship, it's tough to be separated, which probably explains why more and more people are finding ways to include their dogs in their day-to-day work routines. I know people from widely diverse professions, from car salesmen to fashion designers, who routinely take their dogs to the office. One powerful couple in the retail business not only takes their Dandie Dinmont to the office each day (where he's been declared office manager), but on every trip to their far-flung empire of some five hundred shops. In fact, they won't sign a new lease at any property that doesn't allow dogs! Many of my film-star clients take their dogs to studio and location shoots, claiming that their best pal's presence keeps them calm and comforted through the stresses of a day's work. One famous star says, "Bobo is the best therapist in town!" Dogs have that extraordinary ability to make people happy.

Of course, taking your dog to work involves giving the same committed care he gets at home: a quiet retreat to call his own, regular meals of his own food, fresh water, and a regularly scheduled walk. Just because he's hanging out at the office doesn't mean his routine should be disrupted. And if he doesn't seem to be enjoying himself, then be a best friend to him and leave him at home.

Sharing the Love

A wonderful thing about dogs is their ability to help other people, particularly those who need the kind of unconditional love that only a dog can give. I've seen faces of children in hospitals and elderly in nursing homes transformed from hopeless to radiant by one visit from a small, wet-nosed pet-assisted therapy dog. Some of the most desperate cases have made miraculous recoveries. Knowing the medical benefits of a dog's loving presence, hospitals and nursing homes routinely open their doors to these pet-assisted therapy dogs. There are a growing number of groups in this country that share their dogs' love with people who have too little in their lives.

Obviously, not just any pet can visit the sick; a dog must be certified and the first step towards that is the American Kennel Club's Canine Good Citizen Test. This certification is open to all breeds, not just purebreds, and if you've followed each training step in this book, there's no doubt your dog will pass with flying colors, and the certificate that he receives will prove to the world that all your hard work was worth it.

Once your dog is a certified Canine Good Citizen, you may decide to move to the next level: certification as a therapy dog. There are many pet-assisted therapy groups across the country who will provide you with information on the requirements for certification. Your veterinarian, the veterinary society in your area, or staff at your local shelter also can give you information and contacts. Once again, certification bears responsibilities. Among your duties will be giving your dog a previsit bath before each hospital trip, plus grooming and any other requirements of the specific hospital you plan to visit. If you have free time, there's no more rewarding way to spend it.

Creating a Superstar

It's hard for an owner to resist showing his dog's special talents for attracting attention, and many owners view their canine kids as the next Benji. I say, "Why not?" Dogs love to learn, they love to perform, and they especially love the praise and attention that follows a super performance. And since dogs also are happiest when working, they're perfect candidates for learning the more complicated exercises that could send them on to superstardom. Teaching an intelligent dog to "roll over and play dead," "sit up and beg," or even just look woebegone when left behind could land him in one of the many television commercials that rely on the appeal of dogs to sell products. One of my clients has been so successful with her dog—a mixed-breed she rescued from the streets—that her own acting career has taken a backseat to managing his. Her devotion is paying off handsomely in the form of television commercials, movie gigs, and a bright and seemingly limitless theatrical future. If you think your pet has star quality, then by all means, check out my website at www.starpet.com.

Together Forever

The relationship I developed early in life with guard dogs in the internment camp gave me the determination to live life to the fullest. The love and companionship of dogs saw me through the rough times, opened my senses and feelings to new horizons, and set me on the path to reaching them. Later, my relationship with Mariah, the wolf, taught me a new form of communication with animals which created the strongest bond I have experienced on this earth—the bond between man and his friends, the animals. I learned empathy, sensitivity, compassion, and the ability to love unconditionally. From that came my passionate desire to share my newfound gift with others. That passion became my career and, to this day, each new dog I meet, each DogSpeak lesson I give, each owner who learns to communicate with his dog in its own language, gives me an unimaginable feeling of joy in knowing that one more wonderful relationship is being formed.

I take great pleasure in seeing that no dog/owner relationship is a bad one, no problem unsolvable. Even with dogs that may, at first, seem to be a wrong choice, there usually is a right and happy ending which comes from mutual communication through DogSpeak. I hope that, with this book, I've been able to share some of the knowledge that will lead you to this unboundedly joyous relationship. And I know that, from your dog, you will learn the honesty, purity, grace, generosity, and love they have, and give so easily. Then, with their example to inspire us, we all can move forward together to be an example to others, in a better world where all people and all animals live in peace together. We will find the peaceable kingdom at last!

May your life with your dog be long and happy, and may you find, through DogSpeak, the rewards of living with another, quite different but oh-so-remarkable creature.

Appendix

The AKC Canine Good Citizen Test is a terrific way to assess your dog's perfect-manners behavior. The test is open to purebred and mixed-breed dogs alike, and dogs are evaluated in simulated everyday situations involving people and other dogs. Once a dog has completed the test successfully, he becomes a certified Canine Good Citizen. It's enough to make any owner proud!

*AKC Canine Good Citizen Test**

Test 1: Accepting a Friendly Stranger

This test demonstrates that the dog will allow a friendly stranger to approach it and speak to the handler in a natural, everyday situation. The evaluator and handler shake hands and exchange pleasantries. The dog must show no sign of resentment or shyness, and must not break position or try to go to the evaluator.

Test 2: Sitting Politely for Petting

This test demonstrates that the dog will allow a friendly stranger to touch it while it is out with its handler. The dog should sit at the handler's side as the evaluator approaches and begins to pet the dog on the head and body only. The dog must stand in place to accept petting. The dog must not show shyness or resentment.

Test 3: Appearance and Grooming

This practical test demonstrates that the dog will welcome being groomed and examined and will permit a stranger, such as a veterinarian, groomer, or friend of the owner, to do so. It also demonstrates the owner's care, concern, and sense of responsibility. The evaluator inspects the dog, then combs or brushes the dog and lightly examines the ears and each front foot.

Test 4: Out for a Walk (Walking on a Loose Leash)

This test demonstrates that the handler is in control of the dog. The dog may be on either side of the handler, whichever the handler prefers. There must be a left turn, a right turn, and an about turn, with at least one stop in between and another at the end. The dog need not be perfectly aligned with the handler and need not sit when the handler stops.

Test 5: Walking Through a Crowd

This test demonstrates that the dog can move about politely in pedestrian traffic and is under control in public places. The dog and handler walk around and pass close to several people (at least three). The dog may show some interest in the strangers, without appearing overexuberant, shy, or resentful. The handler may talk to the dog and encourage or praise the dog throughout the test. The dog should not be straining at the leash.

Test 6: Sit and Down on Command/Staying in Place

This test demonstrates that the dog has training, will respond to the handler's command to sit and down, and will remain in the place commanded by the handler (sit or down position, whichever the handler prefers). The handler may take a reasonable amount of time and use more than one command to make the dog sit and then down. When instructed by the evaluator, the handler tells the dog to stay and walks forward the length of a twenty-foot line. The dog must remain in place, but may change positions.

Test 7: Coming When Called

This test demonstrates that the dog will come when called by the handler. The handler will walk ten feet from the dog, turn to face the dog, and call the dog. The handler may use encouragement to get the dog to come. Handlers may choose to tell dogs to "stay" or "wait," or they may simply walk away, giving no instructions to the dog as the evaluator provides mild distractions (e.g., petting).

Test 8: Reaction to Another Dog

This test demonstrates that the dog can behave politely around other dogs. Two handlers and their dogs approach each other from a distance of about ten yards, stop, shake hands and exchange pleasantries, and continue on for about five yards. The dogs should show no more than a casual interest in each other.

Test 9: Reactions to Distractions

This test demonstrates that the dog is confident at all times when faced with common distracting situations, such as the dropping of a large book or a jogger running in front of the dog. The dog may express a natural interest and curiosity and/or appear slightly startled, but should not panic, try to run away, show aggressiveness, or bark.

Test 10: Supervised Separation

This test demonstrates that a dog can be left with a trusted person, if necessary, and will maintain its training and good manners. Evaluators are encouraged to say something like, "Would you like me to watch your dog?" and then take hold of the dog's leash. The owner will go out of sight for three minutes. The dog does not have to stay in position but should not continually bark, whine, or pace unnecessarily, or show anything stronger than mild agitation or nervousness.

 To order your free information kit or to purchase test kits, contact:

The American Kennel Club
Attn: CGC
5580 Centerview Drive
Raleigh, NC 27606
(919) 233-9767

If you have any questions about the AKC's Canine Good Citizen Program, please call the AKC's Canine Good Citizen Department at (919) 854-0159 or e-mail CGC@AKC.org.

Index

Page numbers in italic refer to illustrations.